COLLECTED POEMS

COLLECTED POEMS

Alan Dugan

Yale University Press
New Haven, 1969

See acknowledgments for information concerning earlier
publication.
Library of Congress catalog card number: 76–89903
Standard book number (clothbound): 300-0-1118-0
Standard book number (paperbound): 300-0-1119-9
Designed by Marvin Howard Simmons,
set in Garamond type,
and printed in the United States of America by
The Carl Purington Rollins Printing-Office of
the Yale University Press, New Haven, Connecticut.
Distributed in Canada by McGill-Queen's University Press,
Montreal; and in Mexico by Centro Interamericano
de Libros Académicos, Mexico City.

ACKNOWLEDGMENTS

Acknowledgment is made to the following publications for poems which originally appeared in them:

Poetry: Prison Song; Oasis; The Natural Enemies of the Conch; Imperial Song for Warmth; The Branches of Water or Desire; Portrait ("The captive flourished like"); Landfall; Notes Toward a Spring Offensive; Actual Vision of Morning's Extrusion; How We Heard the Name; On an East Wind from the Wars; Philodendron; Three as a Magic Number; To a Redheaded Do-Good Waitress; Winter's Onset from an Alienated Point of View; Free Variation on a Translation from Greek; 851; Fabrication of Ancestors; Admonition: A Pearl for Arrogance; From Heraclitus; On Trees; What the Hell, Rage, Give in to Natural Graces; Variation on a Theme by Stevens; Accommodation to Detroit; Flower Grower in Aquarius; Conspiracy of Two against the World; The Working World's Bloody Flux; His Hands Have Five Knives Each; On Being Out-Classed by Class; Barefoot for a Scorpion; Poem ("Oh that was not a scrap of flying *Daily News*"); Poem ("Flowering balls"); Variation on Themes by Roethke and Eliot; On Rape Unattempted; On Zero

Accent: Love Song: I and Thou; On Hurricane Jackson; Poem ("The person who can do")

The New Yorker: The Stutterer

Cross-Section 1947, ed. Edwin Seaver: Sixteen Lines on Marching

Partisan Review: For Masturbation

Saturday Review: Monologue of a Commercial Fisherman; In the Forest

American Scholar: Winter: For an Untenable Situation

SPEKTRUM (Zürich): Romance of the Escaped Children, translated into German by Annemarie Schönholzer

Jeopardy: Night Song for a Boy

New American Review: Idyll of Ascension

The New York Review of Books: Expenses

The Poetry Bag: Poem ("It is no wonder that new lovers run"); Against Solitude, now retitled "American against Solitude"; Nostalgia for a Language; Poem ("On the old bridge, the bridge"), retitled "Advertising in Paris"; A Hope against Polution

Wascana Review: Poem ("The tree was wet with the moon's"); Brutalization under the Heart of Peace; Northern Statement for St. Cecilia

FOR JUDY

CONTENTS

POEMS

This is this morning: all
the evils and glories of last night
are gone except for their
effects: the great world wars
I and II, the great marriage
of Edward the VII or VIII
to Wallis Warfield Simpson and
the rockets numbered like the Popes
have incandesced in flight
or broken on the moon: now
the new day with its famous
beauties to be seized at once
has started and the clerks
have swept the sidewalks
to the curb, the glass doors
are open, and the first
customers walk up and down
the supermarket alleys of their eyes
to Muzak. Every item has
been cut out of its nature,
wrapped disguised as something
else, and sold clean by fractions.
Who can multiply and conquer
by the Roman numbers? Lacking
the Arab frenzy of the zero, they
have obsolesced: the butchers
have washed up and left
after having killed and dressed
the bodies of the lambs all night,

and those who never have seen blood awake
can drink it browned
and call the past an unrepeatable mistake
because this circus of their present is all gravy.

ON AN EAST WIND FROM THE WARS

The wind came in for several thousand miles all night
and changed the close lie of your hair this morning. It
has brought well-travelled sea-birds who forget
their passage, singing. Old songs from the old
battle- and burial-grounds seem new in new lands.
They have to do with spring as new in seeming as
the old air idling in your hair in fact. So new,
so ignorant of any weather not your own,
you like it, breathing in a wind that swept
the battlefields of their worst smells, and took the dead
unburied to the potter's field of air. For miles
they sweetened on the sea-spray, the foul washed off,
and what is left is spring to you, love, sweet,
the salt blown past your shoulder luckily. No
wonder your laugh rings like a chisel as it cuts
your children's new names in the tombstone of thin air.

ON AN OLD ADVERTISEMENT AND AFTER A PHOTOGRAPH BY ALFRED STIEGLITZ

The formal, blooded stallion, the Arabian,
will stand for stud at fifty bucks a throw,
but there is naturally a richer commerce in his act,
eased in this instance by a human palm
and greased with money: the quiver in his haunch
is not from flies, no; the hollow-sounding,
kitten-crushing hooves are sharp and blind,
the hind ones hunting purchase while the fore
rake at the mare's flank of the sky.
Also, the two- or three-foot prick that curls
the mare's lip back in solar ectasy
is greater than the sum of its desiring:
the great helm of the glans, the head
of feeling in the dark, is what spits out,
beyond itself, its rankly generative cream.
After that heat, the scraggled, stallion-legged foal
is not as foolish as his acts: the bucking and
the splayed-out forelegs while at grass
are practices: he runs along her flank
in felt emergencies, inspired by love to be
his own sweet profit of the fee and the desire,
compounded at more interest than the fifty in the bank.

PHILODENDRON

Drinking Song: An Indoor Plant: A Dull Life

GLOSS

The person of this plant with heart-shaped leaves
and off-shot stalks, bending at each knee,
is built of dishwater, cigarette smoke, no
sunlight, and humus mixed with peat-moss. Like
genius, it survives our inattention and the dark,
potted like myself indoors, and goes on growing.
It grows for no known cause that I can find
outside itself, by means of mumbling, flowering
no flowers, no flowers, none for all these years.

Balance and survival: it has
a strategy of elbows as
it breaks its hairy knees
while climbing up the wall
and then juts off again,
shaped like a claw.

Since imagination has the answer to these noes,
imagine it as one of those survivors in the old
swamps, shadowed by the grown, light-headed conifers:
fit for the damps, whose gentlest odor seems
corrosive, mightily akin to older, shadowed ferns,
it might have dropped its pollen in the black
water where the pollen swam, and thus become
perseverant in going on in lust, like us,
and mobile through its young. Even now

Even at its top most
broken elbow, it
must turn uprooted from
its heaven in the air,
and, in going down,
not find it on the floor,

it does move on in time, too, each elbow putting out
a stalk and leaf in faith and doubt, but no
flowers. Who knows what in hell it loves or lacks
as crawler in arrest. Sometimes to water it,
to notice it, to keep it out of the bureau drawer
and trained to climb perennially around itself,
is piety enough toward indoor plants right now
when one is thirsty, too, for rich lost tastes
and light streaming down through amniotic air.

either. Compelled to move
anyhow, it always has
an angle and an out
in going nowhere, all
around itself
in faith and doubt.

Snow that makes graces on a soldier's sleeve
is ordered rain, the crystal wheels
each agony is strapped to in his business:
waiting in the lee of enemies.
The rain that duplicates forever
can make news again,
distinction in each flake,
but snow is not his order, ordering.

The lesser orders, like the ants,
the spiders, and platoons of snow,
make wholes by ruined parts:
frozen in wait, or jungled monkey-wise,
they organize by jeopardies,
atrocious in design.
Oh web, geometry of appetite,
oh darkly ordered, muted ants,
the snow is not in order, ordering.

Fire and ice burn unalike:
the flakes have touches for his skin,
his eyebrows, and the hair
his hand is aped with; what
exasperation of survival that the snow,
with careful walking,
cracks like salt in the boot
or infiltrates more loving warmth.
Baled in rags
and like a haystack, warm at heart,
unhurt he is a center of decay,

but once the heat is hurt,
the snow for lashes, dusted on his eyes,
will fill his wrinkles of fatigue
with tracery, will cover him to death
with tracery, a thread of shuttles
webbed to net a death. Oh air,
diamond of ice,
the wound is mammoth, fixed in glacial ice:
its trivial grimace will bloom
as rotten ice at thaw.

So which is better, to campaign
between the Tropics where
immediate bulbs of sweat
flower in stains on his fatigues
and rot the living, or among
geodesic spiders of ice?
The latter children nest in a grotesque,
but southward, with the butcher ants,
the death does not
go uniformed in flesh all winter long,
far from the monkey's eulogy,
nor do the wheels of snow
bunch in the lee of his crystal ear
and hum the umbra's note:
Earth makes night, snow is black
in ordering his brain to stop.

PRISON SONG

The skin ripples over my body like moon-wooed water,
rearing to escape me. Where would it find another
animal as naked as this one it hates to cover?
Once it told me what was happening outside,
who was attacking, who caressing, and what the air
was doing to feed or freeze me. Now I wake up
dark at night, in a textureless ocean of ignorance,
or fruit bites back and water bruises like a stone:
a jealousy, because I look for other tools to know
with, and another armor, better fitted to my flesh.
So, let it lie, turn off its clues, or try to leave:
sewn on me seamless like those painful shirts
the body-hating saints wore, this sheath of hell
is pierced to my darkness nonetheless: what traitors
labor in my face, what hints they smuggle through
its itching guard! But even in the night it jails,
with nothing but its lies and silences to feed upon,
the jail itself can make a scenery, sing prison songs
and set off fireworks to praise a homemade day.

The so-called wild horses of the water
stumbled all over the boulders
and fell steaming and foaming over
the world's edge down the roaring
white way of the waterfall
into the black pool of the death
of motion at the bottom where
the cold stoned water lay
dense as a diamond of pressure and
the eye of silence stared unmoved
at the world's cavalry falling in
to be the seer not the heard again.

LANDFALL

The curtains belly in the waking room.
Sails are round with holding, horned at top,
and net a blue bull in the wind: the day.
They drag the blunt hulls of my heels awake
and outrigged by myself through morning seas.
If I do land, let breakfast harbor me.

Waking in June, I found a first fruit
riding out the water on a broken branch.
Sleep was a windfall, and its floating seeds
steered me among the Cyclades of noise.
A coastal woman with a cricket in her hair
took soundings as the time chirped in her head:
I knew that night-time is an Island District;
curtains are my sails to shore.
Block and tackle string a butcher's dance
to hoist the sun on home: the bull
is beached and hung to dry, and through
his bloody noon, the island of his flank
quakes in the silence and disturbs the flies.

Flesh has crawled out on the beach of morning,
salt-eyed, with the ocean wild in hair,
and landed, land-locked, beached on day,
must hitch its hand to traces and resist
the fierce domestic horses teamed to it.

Drivers and driven both, the plowing heels
bloody the furrows after plunging beasts:
the spring of day is fleshed for winter fruit.
Fallen in salt-sweat, piercing skin, the bones
essay plantation in their dirt of home

and rest their aching portion in the heat's
blood afternoon. O if the sun's day-laborer
records inheritable yield, the script
is morning's alpha to omega after dark:
the figured head to scrotum of the bull.

Accountancy at sundown is the wine of night:
walking the shore, I am refreshed by it
and price the windrise and the bellowing surf
while, waiting for its freight of oil and hides,
a first sail starts the wind by snapping whips.

SIXTEEN LINES ON MARCHING

In spring when the ego arose from the genitals
after a winter's refrigeration, the sergeants
were angry: it was a time of looking
to the right and left instead of straight ahead.

Now the rich lost tastes have been lost again,
the green girls grown brown for another year:
intelligent bodies make ready for the entropy begun
by north winds and the declination of the sun.

Say death, soldiering, or fear: these words
are luxuries no more but the true words of winter
when the flesh hardens and collects itself around
the skeleton to protect what little it contains.

If anything is to happen let it happen now.
If anything is expected of us let the orders be cut
immediately and read Winter; the proper season
for caution. Match, if you can, its coldness: spring.

LOVE SONG: I AND THOU

Nothing is plumb, level, or square:
   the studs are bowed, the joists
are shaky by nature, no piece fits
   any other piece without a gap
or pinch, and bent nails
   dance all over the surfacing
like maggots. By Christ
   I am no carpenter. I built
the roof for myself, the walls
   for myself, the floors
for myself, and got
   hung up in it myself. I
danced with a purple thumb
   at this house-warming, drunk
with my prime whiskey: rage.
   Oh I spat rage's nails
into the frame-up of my work:
   it held. It settled plumb,
level, solid, square and true
   for that great moment. Then
it screamed and went on through,
   skewing as wrong the other way.
God damned it. This is hell,
   but I planned it, I sawed it,
I nailed it, and I
   will live in it until it kills me.
I can nail my left palm
   to the left-hand crosspiece but
I can't do everything myself.
   I need a hand to nail the right,
a help, a love, a you, a wife.

1

The first point of the shell
was moored to zero but
its mouth kissed one
and paid in torque.
A turbine in the conch
is whirled so fast
that it stands still,
humming with cold light.

2

The animal inside
is out of luck in art.
Tourists gouge him out
of water's Gabriel
and gild the whirling horn
to make a lamp of home.
The death, a minor surf,
sounds in the living room.

3

(That's the way it is
with the ugly: ugliness
should arm their flesh
against the greedy but
they grow such wiles

around the hurt
that estheticians come
with love, apology,
and knives and cut
the beauty from the quick.)

4

The Maya crack the gem
where muscles glue
the palace to the slug
and eat him out. Again
the curio is fleshed
but wrecked like Knossos
with a window down the maze
toward nothing
where a bull at heart
roars in the start of surf.

5

(To know why slime
should build such forts,
challenge the tooth
one pod is spurred with.
He has a tongue on guard,
like authors, out around
the works, and can retreat

17

in what reveals him,
claw last, at a touch.)

6

Turned in his likeness
like a foraging son,
there is a Natural Drill
that bores a vent in him
and taps his life.
Like Prince Hippolytus,
when we behave too
simply toward some law
we have our image,
father, from the sea:
the sea-bull bellowing
to foul our traces,
dragging us to death
behind disturbed machines.

7

The snail retreats to nothing
where the shell is born,
pearl of its phlegm and rock,
small as water can whirl.
Whorling down the turns
from mouth to point,

it points in vanishing
to university,
where thickened water learned
one graph with nebulae
and turned the living horn
on zero's variable lathe.

8

It voids the plum, wrack
and accidents of space
and sounds a sea-bull
first ashore. Similar ears,
listening mouth to mouth,
hear it as ocean's time
and turn into the brain
as mirrors of the maze.

The seed of an iron flower
must grow in gravel
or else make its own
if it is taken from the desert
and sunk in loam.
What a hard garden,
lovers: iron is used
to the routine of oil
but gets the bloody rust
in damp: there, the oasis,
a devotion in the sand,
prays flesh, virus to mammoth,
and supports them all,
but when the regular iron
flowers in sensuous ease
it languishes; the bloom
weeps dust. Spear-shaped,
venomous as plows were thought to be,
the leaves fall sick
and make a desert: iron's
oasis in delight
and field of strength.

OASIS

Whelped from blackness by a pressure of rocks,
black water rose like breath from the lungs
and burst in speech. It poured its glitter,
trouble, on the sand, and babbled on about
its quick exploits in shape above the plain.
This speaking taught the desert thirst: once
sucked at by that thirster, sand, the water spread
its cool hair over fever: sand was changed:
what was almost sand in sand, the waiting sand,
a hidden seed, leaped up and burst in palms!
The water argued greenery to sand: now sand
is passionate with fruit! Ticking with bugs,
bustling with flowers and death, the garden is
a place and fireworks, a green wild on the calm.

Oh its mirages offer water, figs, and shade
to windrift birds for songs and wings of praise.
Clock-lost nomads, lost in the running sands,
will have to choose, when madness lights
advertisements of water to their soaking need,
if they will drop to the truth of desert, dry
to sand, or run to where the fanfare of quick
water winds their clocks, gives place to love,
and lets them drink their living from its deaths.

PORTRAIT

The captive flourished like
a mushroom in his oubliette.
He breathed his night's breath every day,
took food and water from the walls
and ruled his noisy rats and youth.
He made a calendar of darkness,
thought his boredom out, and carved
Heaven in his dungeon with a broken spoon.

At last he made his own
light like a deep sea fish, and when
his captors' children came for him
they found no madman in a filthy beard
or heap of rat-picked bones:
they found a spry, pale old gentleman
who had a light around his head.
Oh he could stare as well as ever,
argue in a passionate voice
and walk on to the next
detention in their stone dismay
unaided.

The waiter waited, the cook ate,
the scales read zero, and the clock
began to agree. It agreed
and disagreed but rang no bells,
and in the quiet of the whole
peeled onion on the chopping block
the whole flayed lamb stamped
QUALITY
hung by its heels and was
devoured by a fly. Outside,
a woman screamed and stopped.
Two cops came in for coffee-and,
laughing and filling the place
with night as black as the sweat
in the armpits of their shirts.
"Some guy hit his girl friend
and she didn't like it or us
either." Oh it had been
the countdown for a great
catastrophe that had not
happened, not as raw event,
but as time in the death of the lamb.

Now his nose's bridge is broken, one eye
will not focus and the other is a stray;
trainers whisper in his mouth while one ear
listens to itself, clenched like a fist;
generally shadowboxing in a smoky room,
his mind hides like the aching boys
who lost a contest in the Panhellenic games
and had to take the back roads home,
but someone else, his perfect youth,
laureled in newsprint and dollar bills,
triumphs forever on the great white way
to the statistical Sparta of the champs.

POEM

The person who can do
accounts receivable as fast
as steel machines and out-
talk telephones, has wiped
her business lipstick off,
undone her girdle and belts,
and stepped down sighing from
the black quoins of her heels
to be the quiet smiler with
changed eyes. After long-
haired women have unwired
their pencil-pierced buns, it's an
event with pennants when
the Great Falls of emotion say
that beauty is in residence,
grand in her hotel of flesh,
and Venus of the marriage manual,
haloed by a diaphragm,
steps from the shell *Mercenaria*
to her constitutional majesty
in the red world of love.

Imagine that the fast life of a bird
sang in the branches of the cold
cast-off antlers of a stag
and lit the points of bone
with noises like St. Elmo's fire.
Worn, those antlers were
an outer counterweight,
extravagant in air and poised
against a branching need
drumming in the red inside
the arteries or antlers of the heart.
That was the balance that allowed
the stag's head's limber rise,
and might have been the gift
the temporary, reed-boned bird
sang air about: abundance,
rank beyond the need. The horns
appear before the eye to be
more permanent than songs
that branch out lightly on the air
or root into the chest
as singing's negative, the breath,
that touches at the branching veins
at depth:
but when the leaping rut
slept growing in the hollow of the hind,
the candelabra that the head
dazzled the wedding with
guttered to rubbish and were cast.
That perch for calls and bird-
song was a call itself,

and fell to grace the wilds
correctly, since an itch,
under the rootholds of the horns,
whitens with mushroom wants
in cellars of the antlers' nerves
just off the brain,
and wants to make its many points again.

Once cast, they are the dead and fall
duly as a sound falls in the cool
of smoking days, when air
sags with the damp and song
swirls in the hollows: this
is so the works can start again,
untrammeled by the done, downed
wonders, and be upstart news
to publicize the crocus of next spring.
The stag had something on his mind
beside his wants, and it
is more than curious, the way
the horns are worn at ease
by cranial fulcrums, since the like of them,
the lighter songs or battle-cries of birds,
hum in the chambers of the nose
just off the brain,
so that the chambered mute, the brain,
silent in wants and plans,
vibrates in closest sympathy
with what is not its own
and plays as best it can.

Those were the works,
the prides and hat-trees of the head
that climbed out of the brain
to show its matter: earth, and how a beast
who wears a potted plant, all thorns,
is mostly desert, plus a glory
unsustained. Oh it
is useless in a fight
won by the head and heels,
not nicety, not war-cries worn
in silence to be seen. The hinds,
cropping the perimeter of war,
sooner accept the runnel one
who has not fronded his desire
with public works. Call and be gone,
bird: the one who wears the horns
can bear the singer too, mindlessly singing all
the bird-brained airs of spring,
but has to cast the tuning forks
that let the eye see song,
and winter with this loss.

The bone as singing-post
is capital enough in arms
to hold the nation of your sound
in singing's fief: the brain's
savage receptionist, the ear,
beating a drum outside its closest door,
joins with the civil eye's
electrical distance from the brain
in witnessing the poles of prongs and sounds

arcing across their earthworks of desire:
the sounds and tines
must be some excess of the flesh
that wants beyond efficiency
in time, but cannot find
much permanence outside it: getting or not aside,
it must branch out in works
that cap itself, for some
imaginary reason out of mind.

I see that there it is on the beach. It is
ahead of me and I walk toward it: its
following vultures and contemptible dogs
are with it, and I walk toward it. If,
in the approach to it, I turn my back
to it, then I walk backwards: I
approach it as a limit. Even if I fall
to hands and knees, I crawl to it.
Backwards or forwards I approach it.

There is the land on one hand, rising, and
the ocean on the other, falling away;
what the sky does, I can not look to see,
but it's around, as ever, all around.
The courteous vultures move away in groups
like functionaries. The dogs circle and stare
like working police. One wants a heel
and gets it. I approach it, concentrating so
on not approaching it, going so far away
that when I get there I am sideways like
the crab, too limited by carapace to say:

"Oh here I am arrived, all; yours today."
No: kneeling and facing away, I will
fall over backwards in intensity of life
and lie convulsed, downed struggling,
sideways even, and should a vulture ask
an eye as its aperitif, I grant it,
glad for the moment wrestling by a horse
whose belly has been hollowed from the rear,
who's eyeless. The wild dog trapped in its ribs
grins as it eats its way to freedom. Not
conquered outwardly, and after rising once,
I fall away inside, and see the sky around
rush out away into the vulture's craw
and barely can not hear them calling, "Here's one."

PORTRAIT

He wore the burnt-cork moustache and coonskin cap
that all the other boy pirate captains wore
in the comic strips, and when he smiled, real
Douglas Fairbanks diamonds glittered in his eyes
and teeth, but the first mate knew that he
was worried about his father: the fine old
gentleman, chuckling, firm, but kind,
had not been seen for several episodes.
Then it became clear: behind his smiles
and flashing gallantry there were two
serious drives: 1. Concern for the lost father,
and: 2. Worship of fuel as a god,
whether of gas or air, to drive or sail
him forward, always forward in the search,
although the old man had been dropped astern.

The chorus of the weeds, unnameably
profuse, sings Courage, Courage, like
an India of unemployables who have
no other word to say and say it.
Too bendable to break, bowing away
together from the wind although
the hail or hurricane can knock them flat,
they rise up wet by morning. This
morning erection of the weeds
is not so funny: It
is perseverance dancing: some of them,
the worst, are barely rooted and
a lady gardener can pull them out
ungloved. Nevertheless, they do do
what they do or die, surviving all
catastrophes except the human: they
extend their glosses, like the words I said,
on sun-cracked margins of the sown
lines of our harrowed grains.

Ireland was better in its dream,
with the oppressor foreign.
Now its art leaves home to keen
and its voice is orange.
It is a sad revolt, for loving's health,
that beats its enemy and then itself.

Now that Irishmen are free
to enslave themselves together
they say that it is better they
do worst to one another
then have the english do them good
in an exchange of joy for blood.

A just as alien pius blacks
their greens of lovers' commerce;
rehearsing victory, they lack
a government to fill its promise.
Worse, law has slacked the silly harp
that was their once and only Ark

out, and I am sorry to be flip
and narrowly disrespectful,
but since I wade at home in it
I stoop and take a mouthful
to splatter the thick walls of their heads
with American insult! Irish sense is dead.

I guess there is a garden named
"Garden of Love." If so, I'm in it:
I am the guesser in the garden.
There is a notice by the central pond
that reads: "Property of Narcissus.
Trespass at your own risk,"
so I went there. That is where,
having won but disdained a lady,
he fell for his own face and died,
rightly, "not having followed through,"
as the sentence read, read by the lady:
Oh you could hear her crying all about
the wilderness and wickedness of law.
I looked in that famous mirror perilous
and it wasn't much: my own face,
beautiful, and at the bottom,
bone, a rusty knife, two beads,
and something else I cannot name.
I drank my own lips on the dare
but could not drink the lips away.
The water was heavy, cool, and clear,
but did not quench. A lady laughed
behind my back; I learned the worst:
I could take it or leave it, go or stay,
and went back to the office drunk,
possessed of an echo but not a fate.

The lion and lioness are intractable,
the leaves are covered with dust,
and even the peacocks will not
preen. You should come back,
burnish us with your former look,
and let the search for truth
go. After a loud sleep last night
I got up late and saw a new
expression on the faces of the deer;
the shrews and wolves are gaunt
and out of sorts: they nosed
their usual fruits and do not know
what they intend to do. The dogs
got tangled up in an unusual way:
one put its urinary tube
into the other's urinary tract
and could not get it out.
Standing tail to tail for hours,
they looked at me with wise,
supplicatory eyes. I named
two new sounds: snarl and shriek,
and hitherto unnoticed bells,
which used to perform the air,
exploded!, making a difference.
Come back before the garden does
what I'll call "die," not that it
matters. Rib, Rib, I have a new
opinion of your Eve, called "lust"
or Love, I don't know which,
and want to know how I will choose.

AGAINST FRANCE: ON THE ALGERIAN
PLEASURES OF ENTITY

When I died the devils tortured me with icepicks and pliers
and all the other instruments they learned from men of faith;
they took off my genitals and nails, less troubles, chained me
to the wall, and came in shifts with forced foods and electrodes.

Later, after works, I tore the chains from the wall. What whips
chains are! I lashed my lashers and escaped their cell,
armed to my last two teeth in search of god. My arms, though,
were chains chained to my arms, so what I touched I struck.

I met all the animals with beaks and offered them myself
to rend, since, as a student of torture, I had found it fun,
and wrecked them as they bit. What would I have done
if I had met a smile? Well, I swam the river of spit,

crossed a plain of scorpions, and went into the lake
of fire. I emerged bone, dripping the last of my flesh,
a good riddance, and asked whoever came to chew the bones,
"Where is god?" Each answered: "Here I am, now. I am,

in a way." I answered, "Nonsense!" every time and struck
with chains. Weary, weary, I came to the final ocean of acid:
pain was a friend who told me I was temporal when nothing
else spoke, so I dipped in my hand-bones and saw them eaten.

"It is good to be rid of the bones," I felt, "as clattering
encumbrances to search," and dived in whole. However,

instead of being shriven or freed up into flight, oh I
was born again. I squalled for a while to keep my death,

that time when chains were arms and pain a great ally,
but I was conquered and began my sentence to a child's
forgetfulness, uneager to collect the matter of these dreams,
and stared into the present of you innocent beasts.

FUNERAL ORATION FOR A MOUSE

This, Lord, was an anxious brother and
a living diagram of fear: full of health himself,
he brought diseases like a gift
to give his hosts. Masked in a cat's moustache
but sounding like a bird, he was a ghost
of lesser noises and a kitchen pest
for whom some ladies stand on chairs. So,
Lord, accept our felt though minor guilt
for an ignoble foe and ancient sin:
the murder of a guest
who shared our board: just once he ate
too slowly, dying in our trap
from necessary hunger and a broken back.

Humors of love aside, the mousetrap was our own
opinion of the mouse, but for the mouse
it was the tree of knowledge with
its consequential fruit, the true cross
and the gate of hell. Even to approach
it makes him like or better than
its maker: his courage as a spoiler never once
impressed us, but to go out cautiously at night,
into the dining room—what bravery, what
hunger! Younger by far, in dying he
was older than us all: his mobile tail and nose
spasmed in the pinch of our annoyance. Why,
then, at that snapping sound, did we, victorious,
begin to laugh without delight?

Our stomachs, deep in an analysis
of their own stolen baits
(and asking, "Lord, Host, to whom are we the pests?"),
contracted and demanded a retreat
from our machine and its effect of death,
as if the mouse's fingers, skinnier
than hairpins and as breakable as cheese,
could grasp our grasping lives, and in
their drowning movement pull us under too,
into the common death beyond the mousetrap.

I. ENIGMA: CALM: ADDRESSED TO THE AIR

There is the grass to play
with, standing as stiff as nails.

A piece of paper which
was rattled for a week
limps in the lounging air.

Even this breath, all wind
down to the purple lungs
can not blow up a breeze
to clear us out of here.

II. COMMENT ON I.

Here there are armored snails
climbing the grass-blades single file.
Certain as ironclads and as dumb,
they try the heights between
the razor edges of the salt grass
and come a cropper: up
there at the grasses' tips,
swaying in windlessness,
they have to fall. What
will happen to us all
while smothered by the air's
inaction? Slow ourselves,
and waiting for a wind to rise,
we must expect disaster, but
the air is not a savior, iron not

a damned good armor for a fool,
though even love becomes
a doldrum in the tidal
salt-flats of what's beautiful.

The river brought down
dead horses, dead men
and military debris,
indicative of war
or official acts upstream,
but it went by, it all
goes by, that is the thing
about the river. Then
a soldier on a log
went by. He seemed drunk
and we asked him Why
had he and this junk
come down to us so
from the past upstream.
"Friends," he said, "the great
Battle of Granicus
has just been won
by all of the Greeks except
the Lacedaemonians and
myself: this is a joke
between me and a man
named Alexander, whom
all of you ba-bas
will hear of as a god."

Look, it's morning, and a little water gurgles in the tap.
I wake up waiting, because it's Sunday, and turn twice more
than usual in bed, before I rise to cereal and comic strips.
I have risen to the morning danger and feel proud,
and after shaving off the night's disguises, after searching
close to the bone for blood, and finding only a little,
I shall walk out bravely into the daily accident.

Singing, always singing, he was something
of a prig, like Rilke, and as dangerous
to women. They butchered him; but loud
as ever, wanted or not, the bloody head
continued singing as it drifted out to sea.

Always telling, brave in counsel, ruthlessly glib,
he tamed that barbarous drunk, Dionysus,
out of his ecstasy, and taught the Greeks,
once dirt to the gods and damned to hell,
to pray for heaven, godhood, and himself.

O Maenads, who could choke off his revolt?
Shrined as an oracle, the lovely head
went on with its talking, talking, talking,
until the god, the jealous Apollo himself,
came down in a rage and shut it off.

The party is going strong.
The doorbell rings. It's
for someone named me.
I'm coming. I take
a last drink, a last
puff on a cigarette,
a last kiss at a girl,
and step into the hall,
                              bang,
shutting out the laughter. "Is
your name you?" "Yes."
"Well come along then."
"See here. See here. See here."

NOTES TOWARD A SPRING OFFENSIVE

I will begin again in May, describing weather, how
the wind swept up the dust and pigeons suddenly. Then
the rain began to fall on this and that, the regular
ablutions. The soldiers marched, the cowards wept,
and all were wetted down and winded, crushed.
Soldiers turn the dew to mud. Shivering uncontrollably
because the mild wind blew through wet fatigues,
they fell down in the mud, their pieces fouled,
and groveled in the wilderness, regardless. Some died, and how
I will not tell, since I should speak of weather. Afterwards
the clouds were stripped out of the sky. Palpably fresh,
suckingly sweet like bitten peaches, sparkling like oh,
a peeling tangerine, the air was warmed by light again,
and those who could rise rose like crushed chives from the mud
and stank and thought to dry. The cowards wept
and some got well again, profane with flowers, all was well,
and I have finished now in May. I have described
one circle of a day and those beneath it, but not why.

TRANSCRIBED CONVERSATION IN
PRAISE OF COWS

While it is so that you
can eat a pig from nose
to asshole and beyond,
the cow is usefuller:
the beef, beefsteak, broth,
are healthy, and the milk,
the fine glue from the hooves,
the leather and the horns,
Oh you can take one horn
and blow it and call up
whole armies of believers!

Gray smoke rose from the morning ground
and separated into spheres. The smoke
or fog of each sphere coiled upon itself
like snakes at love, and hardened into brains:
the corals in the ocean of first light.
These brains grew shells. Mother of pearl, out
clattered the bones! Two ivies intertwined
ran down them searchingly, the red and white
of arteries and nerves, and found their ends.
Nerves hummed in the wind: the running blood,
in pulsing out a heart, induced a warm,
red haze of flesh around a hollow tube,
writhing with appetite, ejection, love,
and hardened in the temperature of dawn.
"Done!" said the clocks, and gave alarm.
Eyes popped into heads as tears amazed.
All hair stood out. All moved and rose
and took a breath: two gasping voids
turned blue with it around the heart.
Shocked into teeth and nails and wrapped
in winding sheets of skin, all souls walked
to test their creatures in their joints,
chinks, and armors as the walking dead,
curious as to what the water, partial sun-light,
ground and mobile air, combined
reactively, could have in mind.

LIFE COMPARISON

Picked up, a hermit crab who seems
to curl up in a dead snail's shell
from cowardice, attacks the thumb
sustaining him in extraordinary air,
regardless, and if he is attacked
by borers or the other enemies of shells,
he crawls out, raw at the rear!,
to find a new place, thus exposed.
So, he does what is appropriate
within his means, within a case,
and fails: oh he could not bite off
the top whorl of my fingerprint,
although he tried. Therefore, I put
him back to sea for courage, for
his doing what he thinks he has to do
while shrinking, and to propitiate
my own incommensurate enemies,
the firms, establishment, and state.

COOLED HEELS LAMENT AGAINST FRIVOLITY,
THE MASK OF DESPAIR

Dugan's deathward, darling: you
in your unseeable beauty, oh
fictitious, legal person, need
be only formally concerned,
but there is someone too much here,
perspiring in your waiting room.
Because I did not listen when you said,
"Don't call us: we'll call you,"
your credulous receptionist
believes I am a phony fairy jew
capitalist-communist spy
for Antichrist, a deviated mal-
adjusted lobbyist for the Whiskey Trust,
or else accepts me as I am: a fool.
So while I sit here fouling song,
wasting my substance on the air,
the universe is elsewhere, out
the window in the sky. You,
in your inner office, Muse,
smoking a given, good cigar
and swapping dated stories with
star salesmen of the soul,
refuse to hear my novel pitch
while I sit out here getting old.

Rage, closest to reason in the mind,
be cold and smile: you can. The smile of rage
is politic and curls with clarity,
though darker than the black hulk of a tooth,
drumming with ache behind a corner of the lips
that smile to ask the apple-cheek of innocence
up Molars' Alley. So, bite. It snaps against
the pit and hard heart of the ripest fruit
and grows a fast tree barked with pain.
Reason, however, chooses, eats, and spits
external forests for its piece of gain.

So, rage will suffer and do harms,
but may it never be extracted from the face
its beast is manned with: lacking rage,
a mouth falls in upon itself in fear,
the furthest from the reason in the mind,
and sucks its own cheek in to chew
blood's living from the fruits of time.
Reason, closest to rage in the mind,
what can you do but loiter in the mean?,
whose golden apples might offend design
but hang there edibly, while civic teeth
gnash at our only air and latest wild,
and keep their fear of reasoning in mind.

PORTRAIT FROM THE INFANTRY

He smelled bad and was red-eyed with the miseries
of being scared while sleepless when he said
this: "I want a private woman, peace and quiet,
and some green stuff in my pocket. Fuck
the rest." Pity the underwear and socks,
long burnt, of an accomplished murderer,
oh God, of germans and replacements, who
refused three stripes to keep his B.A.R.,
who fought, fought not to fight some days
like any good small businessman of war,
and dug more holes than an outside dog
to modify some Freudian's thesis: "No
man can stand three hundred days
of fear of mutilation and death." What he
theorized was a joke: "To keep a tight
asshole, dry socks and a you-deep hole
with you at all times." Afterwards,
met in a sports shirt with a round wife, he was
the clean slave of a daughter, a power brake
and beer. To me, he seemed diminished
in his dream, or else enlarged, who knows?,
by its accomplishment: personal life
wrung from mass issues in a bloody time
and lived out hiddenly. Aside from sound
baseball talk, his only interesting remark
was, in pointing to his wife's belly, "If
he comes out left foot first" (the way
you Forward March!), "I am going to stuff
him back up." "Isn't he awful?" she said.

ON AN ARCHITECT

1

A mine is a hollow tree upside-down in the ground:
the galleries branch out into rooms like leaves
facing and feeding off the rock the way the leaves
exert their palms against the air and drink it.
The tree of earth in the air and its reverse,
the tree of air in the earth, grow up and down
until the world comes: "Put everything back as it was."
Then, after the thundering earthquakes and lightning
of the earth in air, they are no longer there in the same
miraculous silence of their having been there,
except for some hollow and some solid trash
and the metaphysical difference surviving in the image.

2

We poured a pulverized mountain of cement
around an orange-painted mineful of iron
and formed it harder than the term
"concrete" when used in metaphysics to
contrast to "nothing." From the squat
cyclopean basements to the rococco heights
it was a dream. "Fuck 'em all!" I said.
"The janitor can run a jacob's ladder up
the Giants' Staircase and put folding chairs
for hire in the Great Hall: let them pee out
the Rose Window if they have to: there is no
plumbing in my monument." It is; it is

an iron tree, concrete in leaf, meant
to cement man's presence to eternity,
and people pay to enter and be small,
but on these hazy, violet days and with
the sun behind it, oh it seems
almost to disappear, so I went up to it
and hit it. "By my forehead's blood,
oh tricky senses, oh Empirical Philosophers,
I wear the ache that proves it to be there
and not, as light reports, a condensation of the air."

LETTER TO DONALD FALL

I walked a hangover like my death down
the stairs from the shop and opened the door
to a spring snow sticking only to the tops
of air-conditioners and convertibles, and thought
of my friend Donald Fall in San Francisco.
Toothless in spring!, old friend, I count
my other blessings after friendship
unencumbered by communion: I have:
a money-making job, time off it, a wife
I still love sometimes unapproachably
hammering on picture frames, my own
city that I wake to, that the snow
has come to noiselessly at night, it's there
by morning, swallowing the sounds of spring
and traffic, and my new false teeth,
shining and raw in the technician's lab
like Grails, saying, "We are the resurrection
and the life: tear out the green stumps
of your aching and put plastic on instead:
immortality is in science and machines."
I, as an aging phony, stale, woozy, and corrupt
from unattempted dreams and bad health habits,
am comforted: the skunk cabbage generates its
frost-thawing fart-gas in New Jersey and the first
crocuses appear in Rockefeller Center's Channel Gardens:
Fall, it is not so bad at Dugan's Edge.

Not even dried-up leaves,
skidding like iceboats on
their points down winter streets,
can scratch the surface of
a child's summer and its wealth:
a stagnant calm that seemed
as if it must go on and on
outside of cyclical variety
the way, at child-height on a wall,
a brick named "Ann"
by someone's piece of chalk
still loves the one named "Al"
although the street is vacant and
the writer and the named are gone.

TRIPTYCH

Scoundrels, Scoundrels

ADAM SMITH	KARL MARX	JESUS CHRIST
Wheat is probably a better food than oats,	But if we are to demand that the rate of profit, say 14.876934. . , should be exactly equal in every business and every year, down to the hundredth decimal place, on pain of degradation to a fiction, we should be grossly misunderstanding the nature of the rate of profit and of economic laws in general—none of them has any reality except as approximation, tendency, average, but not in *immediate* reality.	34. Think not that I am come to send peace on earth. I am not come to send peace, but a sword.
but not than potatoes.		35. For I am come to set a man at variance against his father, and the daughter against her mother, and the daughter-in-law against her mother-in-law.
Potatoes, however, are perishable.	This is partly due to the fact that their action is thwarted by the simultaneous action of other laws, but also in part to their own nature as	

concepts.

Marry. Sweets, tarts and sweets,
come among soots and sherds.
The dairy of the breasts
and warehouse of the balls
will out-last granaries
when grains and futures fall,

granted a lasting. Lust
that lasts a bloodshot night
protected from the air
will breakfast in wrecked day,
excused because it must,
and find its scavenge there.

Given a harvest of wives
and lopping-off of males,
granted that some survive,
the warden of the weak
is number, blood's variety
marauding in the streets.

So, penis, guide the flesh
to shelter in the womb
when sirens and the police
lament all other homes,
and if born, suckling mouths
grow privily with fangs,

59

well, fangs are promises
to live on what is left,
granted some leavings, and
monsters are replies.
So, marry. Sours and sweets
come among shots and cries.

The frantic elk climb from the valleys to escape the flies.
Then, on the heights, they leap, run, and play in snow
as Alces, Alces, glad to be relieved of goads
and ready to get married, due to the wholesome airs.
Those gads downhill, buzzing in armor causative,
must have their joys in cycles too, if the escape
from them in dancing Io!, Io!, on the heights is how,
oh Alces!, Alces!, Hymen triumphs and the roaring stags
fight to assemble harems in the trampled snow
while gad-eggs cradle in their hides and nostrils.

They set out every year diagonally to make
the grand tour of their corner of the world in Oregon,
spurred by a bug at base and climbing up to love
on the apex, and without that lightning touch of Zeus
to slap them, Ha!, Epaphus!, out of the cycling dark
and innocent present of the locally driven beasts,
and toward the widening drive all over Asia and up
into the sky, too, that is the cycle of the really stung.

God help us on a day
like this and one of many.
This day was full
of merciful activity
but we got through
at last to supper: lamb
will be good but do
no good: Christ knows
where it will be
tomorrow down the drain.
Oh it was slaughtered like
himself and hung to dry,
so may we eat it up,
talking in mindless ease,
and by the fishwife,
Mary, star of the sea,
ride out the night
and eat some fish on Friday.

STUTTERER

Courage: your tongue has left
its natural position in the cheek
where eddies of the breath
are navigable calms. Now
it locks against the glottis or
is snapped at by the teeth,
in midstream: it must be work
to get out what you mean:
the rapids of the breath
are furious with belief
and want the tongue, as blood
and animal of speech,
to stop it, block it, or come clean
over the rocks of teeth
and down the races of the air,
tumbled and bruised to death.
Relax it into acting, be
the air's straw-hat
canoeist with a mandolin
yodeling over the falls.
This is the sound advice
of experts and a true despair:
it is the toll to pass the locks
down to the old mill stream
where lies of love are fair.

After hundreds of years of common sense
action appeared at the corners of all eyes:
lights appeared at night, and sounds of war
whammed from the desert back of town.

At first only the outlying saints saw them,
but later they strolled through the streets:
bat-faced devils walking arm in arm
with blond white angels in a tourists' truce.

It was then that Natural Law was repealed
and a public virgin wept that it was she
to whom a fiend or angel had appeared
announcing an unearthly rape of sorts
and the arrival of a difficult child.

ON THE SUPPOSED IMMORALITY OF ORCHIDS

Orchids are poisonous blooms, though
beautiful, because they flower
rootloose on the air and suck,
instead of solid food,
the vicious disposition of the wind.
Paolo!, Francesca!, with no hope
of hold: take heart in air
as sustenance for flight: plants
can root in the uprooting wind
and take, as rationale,
equivocal beauties from thin air.

Trees get choked by their bouquets
but give support. They praise the bloom.
I damn the means.
Praise teaches. In hunting ways
to root in air but succor hosts,
a moral botanist might find
juster symbiotics on the wind:
plants that will pay, for arboring,
a decorative, fair return,
and trees that will survive
the grapples of the flowers.

The men laughed and baaed like sheep
and marched across the flashing day
to the flashing valley. A shaved
pig in a uniform led the way.

I crawled down Old Confusion, hid,
and groaned for years about my crime:
was I the proper coward, they
heroically wrong? I lived out their time!,

a hard labor, convict by look and word:
I was the fool and am penitent:
I was afraid of a nothing, a death;
they were afraid of less, its lieutenant.

WALL, CAVE, AND PILLAR
STATEMENTS, AFTER ASÔKA

In order to perfect all readers
the statements should be carved
on rock walls, on cave walls,
and on the sides of pillars so
the charm of their instruction can
affect the mountain climbers near
the cliffs, the plainsmen near
the pillars, and the city people near
the caves they go to on vacations.

The statements should, and in a fair
script, spell out the right text and gloss
of the Philosopher's jocular remark. Text
"Honesty is the best policy." Gloss:
"He means not 'best' but 'policy,'
(this is the joke of it) whereas in fact
       Honesty is Honesty, Best
       is Best, and Policy is Policy,
       the three terms being not
       related, but here loosely allied.
What is more important is that 'is'
is, but the rocklike truth of the text
resides in the 'the'. The 'the' is The.
       By this means the amusing sage
       has raised or caused to be raised
       the triple standard in stone:
the single is too simple for life,
the double is mere degrading hypocrisy,
but the third combines the first two
in a possible way, and contributes

something unsayable of its own:
this is the pit, nut, seed, or stone
of the fruit when the fruit has been
digested:
>It is good to do good for the wrong
>reason, better to do good for the good
>reason, and best of all to do good
>good: i.e. when the doer and doee
>and whatever passes between them
>are beyond all words like 'grace'
>or 'anagogic insight,' or definitions like
>'particular instance of a hoped-at-law,'
>and which the rocks alone can convey.
This is the real reason for the rock walls,
the cave walls and pillars, and not the base
desires for permanence and display
that the teacher's conceit suggests."

>That is the end of the statements, but,
>in order to go on a way after the end
>so as to make up for having begun
>after the beginning, and thus to come around
>to it in order to include the whole thing,
add: "In some places the poignant slogan,
'Morality is a bad joke like everything else,'
may be written or not, granted that space
exists for the vulgar remarks, the dates,
initials and hearts of lovers, and all
other graffiti of the prisoners of this world."

POEMS 2

THREE AS A MAGIC NUMBER

Three times dark, first in the mind,
second in January, the pit of the year,
and third in subways going up and down
the hills and valleys underground,
I go from indoors to indoors indoors,
seeing the Hudson River three times a week
from my analyst's penthouse window. It
is a brilliant enlargement three ways:
in and out and fluvial. The river goes
like white smoke from the industries
to the north, and the rigged-up lights
of the Palisades Amusement Park
promise a west of pleasure, open space,
and a circus of whippable lions,
while the cliffs beneath them, made
of latent vegetation, the live rock,
and a fall of snow, seems to me to be
the hanging gardens of Hammurabi.

COAT OF ARMS

In memory of E. A. Dugan

My father's Memory Book
was warm before the womb
among gymnasium smells
of resolutions put to dust.
The grand tour of his squint
that stopped for photographs
before each sepia Wonder
found Ithaca and ease
beneath the attic dust.
What a joker, like me:
he came into the womb
where I was, poked around
and spat and left and I
was forced out wet
into the cold air. Someone
slapped me and I wept
to have become a traveling man.
Oh I inherited his book
stamped with a coat of arms
self-made from dreams—
a moon and family beast,
a phrase around a shield
boldly nicked with feats
and warm before the womb—
and wondered, laughing, why,
when heroes have come home
from labors out of time
they loll out fatherhood
in baseball-worship, old

underclothes, odd sales jobs
and bad stories often told,
told often, stories often told,
but in one photograph,
the last before the womb,
the dragon had been stuffed
and shipped off home,
authentically killed, and he
is posed in mail, his head
fixed in a photographer's clamp
and Coney Island smile
graced by the cry: "INHIBIT!"
So I learned to rent arms too,
and go out broke without
escutcheon, with a blank
shield against all critics and
a motto of my own
devising on the rim:

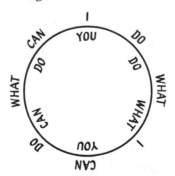

and throw down a left-handed glove
under the cry: "ETCETERA!"

Goodbye, children: the bad Good Knight
is through. The rescued girl is asleep,
dreaming of ransom and astrologers
in the highest room of the family Keep.

On the second floor the Him Himself
is sound asleep among his pudding wife
and in the great Ground Hall below
retainers denounce the family wine

and pick at the bones of a cold dwarf.
Down in the cellars you shivered about,
continuous shrieks applaud the rack: he is,
from top to bottom, a good to bad scout,

domestic in the middle. You are fortunate
to have escaped from this on muffled oars.

ELEGY

I know but will not tell
you, Aunt Irene, why there
are soapsuds in the whiskey:
Uncle Robert had to have
a drink while shaving. May
there be no bloodshed in your house
this morning of my father's death
and no unkept appearance
in the living, since he has
to wear the rouge and lipstick
of your ceremony, mother,
for the first and last time:
father, hello and goodbye.

TWO QUITS AND A DRUM,
AND ELEGY FOR DRINKERS

1. On Asphalt: No Greens

Quarry out the stone
of land, cobble the beach,
wall surf, name it "street,"
allow no ground or green
cover for animal sins,
but let opacity of sand
be glass to keep the heat
outside, the senses in.
Then, when time's Drunk,
reeling to death, provokes
god's favor as a fool,
oh let a lamp post grow
out of its absence, bend,
heavy with care, and bloom
light. Let a curb extrude
a comfortable fault. Let
"street" become a living room.
Comfortably seated, lit
by the solicitude of "lamp,"
the Drunk and street are one.
They say, "Let's have no dirt:
bulldoze the hills into
their valleys: make it plain.
Then take the mountains down
and let their decks of slate
be dealt out flat grey.
Let their mating seams
be tarred against the weeds
by asphalt, by the night's

elixir of volcanoes hotly poured."
Then the soulless port at night
is made a human, and the Drunk
god: no one else is here
to be so but who cares?

2. PORTRAIT AGAINST WOMEN

Bones, in his falling,
must have hit the skin
between themselves and stone,
but distances of wine
were his upholstery
against the painful crime
of lying in the street,
since "God protects them."
He rolled onto his back,
his right hand in his fly,
and gargled open-mouthed,
showing the white of an eye:
it did not see the sign
raised on the proper air
that read: "Here lies
a god-damned fool. Beware."
No: his hand, his woman, on
the dry root of his sex,
debates it: deformed by wine
and fantasy, the wreck
of infant memory is there,

77

of how the garden gate
slammed at the words, "Get
out you god-damned bum,"
and so he was, since she,
goddess, mother, and wife,
spoke and it was the fact.
Her living hair came out
gray in his hand, her teeth
went false at his kiss,
and her solid flesh went slack
like mother's. "Now, lady, I
am sick and out of socks,
so save me: I am pure although
my hand is on my cock."
Then he could rise up young
out of his vagrancy
in whole unwilled reform
and shuck the fallen one,
his furlough in this street
redeemed by her grace.
There would be the grass
to lay her on, the quench
of milk behind the taste of wine,
and laughter in a dreamed
jungle of love behind
a billboard that could read:
"This is YOUR Garden:
Please keep it clean."

3. COURAGE. EXCEED.

A beggar with no legs below
the middle of his knees
walked down Third Avenue
on padded sockets, on
his telescoped or
anti-stilted legs
repeating, "Oh beautiful
faspacious skies!" upon
a one-man band: a bass
drum on roller-skates,
a mouth-high bugle clamped
to it, and cymbals interlocked
inside a fate of noise. He
flew the American flag
for children on a stick
stuck in a veteran's hat,
and offered pencils. He
was made of drunks' red eyes.
He cried, "Courage! Exceed!"
He was collapsed in whole
display. Drunkards, for this
and with his pencil I
put down his words drunk:
"Stand! Improvise!"

4. ELEGY FOR DRINKERS

What happened to the drunks
I used to know, the prodigals

who tried their parents' help
too far? Some misers of health
have aged out dry; the rest
are sick and out of socks,
their skin-tight anklebones
blue as the mussel shells
that rolled in Naxos' surf
when Bacchus danced ashore
and kicked them all to hell.

    Oh gutter urinal,
    be Dirce's holy stream,
    so lightning out of Zeus
    can rage on Semele,
    invited! Permit her son,
    issuant of His thigh,
    to rule her family
    as Bromios, god of wine!

Oh Dionisos, good god
of memory and sleep,
you grace the paper bag,
stuck in the fork of a crutch,
that holds the secret sons
and furniture of bums,
since wine is the cure of wine.
It's thanks to you that I,
in my condition, am
still possible and praising: I
am drunk today, but what
about tomorrow? I burnt

my liver to you for a drink,
so pay me for my praises:
for thirty-seven cents, for
the price of a pint of lees,
I would praise wine, your name,
and how your trouble came
out of the east to Thebes:
you taught the women wine
and tricked King Pentheus
to mask as one of them:
because his father died
to all appeals for help,
the rending penalty,
death at his mother's hands!,
still fills The Bowery
with prodigals of hope:
they pray for lightning and
a dance to their god damn,
since wine is the cure of wine
and wine the cure wine cured
and wine the cure of wine.

TO A RED-HEADED DO-GOOD WAITRESS

Every morning I went to her charity and learned
to face the music of her white smile so well
that it infected my black teeth as I escaped,
and those who saw me smiled too and went in
the White Castle, where she is the inviolable lady.

There cripples must be bright, and starvers noble:
no tears, no stomach-cries, but pain made art
to move her powerful red pity toward philanthropy.
So I must wear my objectively stinking poverty
like a millionaire clown's rags and sing, "Oh I

got plenty o' nuttin'," as if I made
a hundred grand a year like Gershwin, while
I get a breakfast every day from her for two
weeks and nothing else but truth: she has
a policeman and a wrong sonnet in fifteen lines.

Oh I got up and went to work
and worked and came back home
and ate and talked and went to sleep.
Then I got up and went to work
and worked and came back home
from work and ate and slept.
Then I got up and went to work
and worked and came back home
and ate and watched a show and slept.
Then I got up and went to work
and worked and came back home
and ate steak and went to sleep.
Then I got up and went to work
and worked and came back home
and ate and fucked and went to sleep.
Then it was Saturday, Saturday, Saturday!
Love must be the reason for the week!
We went shopping! I saw clouds!
The children explained everything!
I could talk about the main thing!
What did I drink on Saturday night
that lost the first, best half of Sunday?
The last half wasn't worth this "word."
Then I got up and went to work
and worked and came back home
from work and ate and went to sleep,
refreshed but tired by the weekend.

Ephemeron! It's over! All
the scales of the clock-faces
are so heavy with life,
so loaded to capacity
with eyelids and lashes,
that they have come around again
to zero, midnight. Since you
were no Faust at noon,
no Mephistopheles at midnight
will reward your prayers with Hell
and its continuous distractions: it's
just all over, Ephemeron.

COUNTER-ELEGY

Oh no. I go on
doing what I have
to do because I do
it: I sat and sat
there counting one
plus one plus one
while all the rest
were somewhere else,
playing in the tripe
of a living horse
and stroking its great
eyes: this took time!
Then at the end
of that eternity

they gave me 60 bucks
less taxes and dues
and said, "Come back
tomorrow; there
is always work to do."
It was night! I went out!
Oh I got stewed,
screwed and tattooed!
My skin read: I LOVE
MY MOTHER in a heart
pierced by a naked sword!
Weak in the needling, it
was there for all life long
in the bent branch of my arm.
You think I just
went off like a bomb
and was over, but
it has seemed long to me,
slow as the explosion of
the whole life of the tree
in which the birds evolved,
each singing out its song.

CREDO

They told me, "You don't have
to work: you can starve,"
so I walked off my job
and went broke. All day
I looked for love and cash
in the gutters and found
a pencil, paper, and a dime
shining in the fading light,
so I ate, drank, and wrote:
"It is no use: poverty
is worse than work, so why
starve at liberty? when I
can eat as a slave, drink
in the evening, and pay
for your free love at night."

WINTER'S ONSET FROM
AN ALIENATED POINT OF VIEW

The first cold front came in
whining like a carpenter's plane
and curled the warm air
up the sky: winter is
for busy work, summer
for construction. As for
spring and fall, ah, you
know what we do then:
sow and reap. I want
never to be idle or by plumb
or level to fear death,
so I do none of this
in offices away from weather.

ON HAT: ON VERTICAL MOBILITY
AS A CONCEPT

From the official hurry on the top floor
and through the irony on the working floors
down to the sleep stolen in the basement,
the company went on incorporate and firm,
drumming like an engine through the spring day.
Standing still but often going up and down
while breaking in a new winter felt hat,
the elevator operator was the best man in
the place in humor. Going from the thieves
at the top to the bums in the cellar
and past the tame working people in between,
he was denoting Plato's ideal form of Hat
vertically in an unjust state in the spring:
he did nothing but social service for nothing
as a form to be walked on like stairs.

The receptionist has shiny fingernails
since she has buffed them up for hours,
not for profit but for art, while they,
the partners, have been arguing themselves
the further into ruthless paranoia,
the accountant said. The sales representatives
came out against the mustard yellow: "It
looks like baby-shit," and won, as ever. In
the studio, the artist, art director, and
the copy chief were wondering out loud:
Whether a "Peace On Earth" or a "Love
And Peace On Earth" should go around
the trumpeting angel on the Christmas card.
In this way the greeting card company
worked back and forth across a first spring
afternoon like a ferryboat on the river:
time was passing, it itself was staying the same,
and workers rode it on the running depths
while going nowhere back and forth across
the surface of the river. Profits flow away
in this game, and thank god there is none
of the transcendence printed on the product.

FREE VARIATION ON A
TRANSLATION FROM GREEK

In times of peace and good government
there is increase of fruits and ease.
The house-spider tries to spin her web
from the air raid helmet to the gun
in the closet, but quits at the sound
of the morning vacuum cleaner: the sound
father keeps his weapons clean but locked away.
The afternoon is broad. The evening
is for supper and nothing. At night the ex-
soldier can wake from honey-hearted sleep
and turn to his own wife in his own
bed for a change, for solace against fears
of death by normal attrition. At 6 A.M.
there are no police knocking: his only problems,
besides the major ones of love, work, and death,
are noisy children: playing out in the street
before breakfast and against his rules, a joke
occurs, and their laughter starts, builds,
and then goes up like a prayer against the rules
and for the time of peace and good government
in which it happens: they could have lit
a used Christmas tree: it goes up in fire
but burns invisibly in the clear morning air
while roaring. Then he goes to work again,
instead of war, and the day stands as said.

You laughed with an open mouth
to show the flowering ivory
of your temporary teeth because
you hit him on the head hard
with a croquet mallet, drawing
real blood. Now I know you as
the laugher and the hammerer,
as Charles Martel The Churl
who comes to change the past
with blood and laughter. Don't
fall to the grief that makes
your father beat you up, but
encourage your essence! Be-
jewel your mallet and strike
for a world of growing joy.

Arcadia was square and fenced
with upright planks. It had
a slate path pretended as
a stream of square meander
which I hopped and helped
my mother May to cross.
Roses were tied to sticks
in dirty holes in the grass.
Once I saw a snake
and ran away indoors,
crying of hell, and stopped
her conversation with an aunt.
Armored in women, I
returned and found the worm
groveling in laughter: it
had crucified the roses and
had made a fool of snakes
before I did or did not
stamp it out. I fell asleep
and did not wake up later,
until I woke up far away
and worked to be your lover.

FOR MASTURBATION

I have allowed myself
this corner and am God.
Here in the must
beneath their stoop
I will do as I will,
either as act as act,
or dream for the sake of dreams,
and if they find me out
in rocket ships or jets
working to get away,

then let my left great-toe-
nail grow into the inside knob
of my right ankle bone and let
my fingernails make eight new moons
temporarily in the cold salt marches of my palms!
THIS IS THE WAY IT IS, and if
it is "a terrible disgrace"
it is as I must will,
because I am not them
though I am theirs to kill.

Confusedly, I used to think
of the wind as the item
connoting evanescence, and of stone
as the permanent thing, but
stone is blown full of holes
by the wind. The fighters' toes
in the Halicarnassus frieze
are corrupt with the athlete's foot
of many years of endurance,
or with some other wasting power.
Elgin! Where are the penises
and noses? A Captain Hammond
took two heads to Denmark;
other heads cut in half
show how the stone's brains
are full of incidents. Who cares
whether the faces are chopped off
or not? The fine grains of the stone
in the inside of their heads
are full of reasonable patterns.
The stone thought of the stone
figures is thus exposed:

    that the marble is
    processional like its friezes
    of gods, people, and beasts
    and their grasses fed by water
    down from the rock tables

in the mountains where
the marbles came from in
their process from the quarry
to the dust motes in a sunbeam
entering a dead museum
and goes off someplace else
I can not know about while going.

After the victory he loped
through town, still bloodily
unwounded, grinning like a dog
aroused, and with his sword
hanging down from his hand.
The Spartans yelled, "Go screw
What's-her-name just as you are,
crazy and stinking with war!
Her husband will be proud,
or say he is, when she,
yielding, conceives a noble child."

POEM

Whatever was living is dead
and a lot of what was dead
has begun to move around,
so who knows what
the plan for a good state
is: they all go out
on the roads! Wherever
they came from is down,
wherever they're going
is not up yet, and everything
must make way, so,
now is the time to plan
for a new city of man.
The sky at the road's end
where the road goes up
between one hill and ends,
is as blank as my mind,
but the cars fall off
into great plains beyond,
so who knows what
the plan for a good state
is: food, fuel, and rest
are the services, home
is in travel itself,
and burning signs at night
say DYNAFLO! to love,
so everything goes.

ON AN ACCIDENT:
ON A NEWSPAPER STORY

When a child turned in a false
alarm, a deaf man walked in front
of the fire engine. The attraction
between deafness and clangor is so
powerful, and some drivers are so
Christ-like—in saving the one
they damage many—that ten
people went to Coney Island Hospital
to lie as culls of the event among
the other victims of the Whip,
the Cyclone, and the Tunnel of Love.
Children can act largely, death
can be small, and art can go on
from the pains of its individuals.

A flying pigeon hit me on a fall day
because an old clothes buyer's junk cart
had surprised it in the gutter: license 851.
The summer slacks and skirts in the heap
looked not empty and not full of their legs,
and a baseball cap remained in head-shape.
Death is a complete collector of antiques
who finds, takes, and bales each individual
of every species all the time for sale to god,
and I, too, now have been brushed by wings.

FABRICATION OF ANCESTORS

For old Billy Dugan, shot in the ass in the Civil War,
my father said.

The old wound in my ass
has opened up again, but I
am past the prodigies
of youth's campaigns, and weep
where I used to laugh
in war's red humors, half
in love with silly-assed pains
and half not feeling them.
I have to sit up with
an indoor unsittable itch
before I go down late
and weeping to the storm-
cellar on a dirty night
and go to bed with the worms.
So pull the dirt up over me
and make a family joke
for Old Billy Blue Balls,
the oldest private in the world
with two ass-holes and no
place more to go to for a laugh
except the last one. Say:
The North won the Civil War
without much help from me
although I wear a proof
of the war's obscenity.

AUTUMN AT BAIAE: FOR CAVAFY

The women, clients, and slaves wept
and pretended the louder as he read
the temporal restitution of his thefts,
but the men stared: panic and avarice
exploded behind their eyes, shaded
from the candidate for certain lightning.
"Now, being condemned to a glory I
can neither avoid nor survive, I make
my will." Then, like a combat officer
committed for the last time to the point
of fire, M. C. Tacitus drove away
for his two hundred days as Emperor.

RIDING SONG FOR A SEMI-FEUDAL ARMY,
FOR GLUBB PASHA,
FOR TORTURED COLONELS

On a brilliant morning in May
we stole horses and set out
after the enemy (six kibbutzniks
gossiping about their tractors,
tractors and trivia), tired as usual
and dirty, but laughing and talking
of love. Then the poet of the left
flushed a quail, shot it through the eye,
jumped a rock pile, caught it
as it fell, and gave it to the Colonel, saying:

"On a brilliant morning in May
we stole horses and set out
after the enemy (six kibbutzniks
debating the yokelization
of the intelligentsia). We were dirty and tired
as usual, but we laughed and talked
dirtily of love. Then I shot
a bird in the eye, caught it as it fell
so as to save the flesh intact
and gave it to the Colonel, saying:

'Who knows who will be alive
tomorrow? In the meantime I will give
the Colonel the bird to make him
able in strategy, careful in tactics, and
respectful of these lives of ours,
not that they matter: he
deserves a good last supper tonight.' "
The Colonel accepted the gift, laughing,

and turned to the war correspondent
riding beside him and said, "Now

you see why I like to sneak out
of the office and ride with these kids."
"I see," said the reporter. "It is vanity."
"The Colonel got the bird," said the poet.
"And we rode on after the enemy (six
kibbutzniks debating Martin Buber's so-called position),
fooling away our fear and dreaming
of peace and glory at the same time,
which is impossible, though death is not:
the Israelis are anti-romantic."

POEM

In the old days either the plaintiff or the defendant won or lost
justly or unjustly according to the mood of the court; the innocent
and the guilty were acquitted or condemned according to their luck
or pull with justice. Nowadays they are all condemned to death
by hard labor, together with the lawyers, juries, and arresting police.
Then the boards of review condemn the presiding judges, too,
for having wasted time. In this way, all those who are in any way
connected with justice are impartially disconnected, and the clerk
closes the court house to join the last judgement. This is not to say
that there is no more justice: as an only natural human invention to
begin with, it has turned into the needs of the state, which needs labor.
The whole apparatus can be forgotten in the absence of individuals
to whom to apply it, and the sensible man will have nothing to do
with anything outside his inner, passional life except his position.

ON LINES 69–70, BOOK IV,
OF VIRGIL'S *AENEID*

AENEAS: *Then I will found a temple of solid marble to
Phoebus and Trivia.*

You can read the pictures stamped
on the brass door: there
is Aeneas in chin and black boots
doing the Roman salute
as Dido tears at her hair.
The curly waves of the sea
perform close-order drill
while the purple corpse of Pan
disorders the public air
to show that Christ is here.
Long bugles of government
blow to their hearts' content
that honor is murderous.
I even saw Orpheus
sailing in Jason's fleet
and plucking a civic lyre
in praise of colonial fleece.
"That's enough," the priestess said.
"You came here in holy dread
and do not have the time
to laugh at the art any more.
I enlist whatever is mine,
so come in and fill out the forms."

In winter a crow flew at my head
because her fledgling warmed
the brute nest of my fist. Ah,
the pearl clipped in her yellow beak
fell from her cry of "Ransom," and
I freed my bird for grace.

There in the pearl I prophesied
a ball to gaze in, with the stars
mirrored upon it as it held
the image of the crow at core.
Spread-eagled in the royal orb,
the black bird grew, one foot
holding lightning and the other,
worms: a herald arrogance.
I saw my fortune, iridescent
with deceit, my golden mask
the operative profile on a coin
haloed in motto: Order Reigns,
and backed by pestilent wings.

The window in this easter egg
exposed the blood's close tenement
where out-sized eyes, two bright
black pebbles in tarred grass,
were imminent with birth,
and hunger's instrument, the beak,
armored its hinterland of flesh
with bone. It will crack out

of art, the image at full term,
and cast about for meal.

How I hoped for a peaceable bird,
foolish as the gooney or dove!,
that would crack out of will
unhungry but immune to fists,
but I expect some arrogance
in flesh, be it of pigeons
or flightless birds, and do not know
a trustable source of order in
designs. I hear of Yeats' trick,
autocratic in the metal,
and of Picasso's normative dove,
gala with hopes, but what I eat
is this admonitory crow.

Air is the first international
when soldiers smell the girls
and funerals in flowers in
contained wars in spring. They swear
allegiance to the air and are
remobilized for the campaigns
of love nightly, in sexual cells,
subverted by the nose to be
patriots of what is not
or partisans of a rose,
but go on drilling. So, fall out
on sick call for a shot
against the air and go on
killing. A private Eden blooms
like a grenade inside their skulls,
corporal with apples, snakes, and Eves,
exploding outward toward the fall
from summer's marching innocence
to the last winter of general war.

They were always arguing that we
were either the Devil's puppets or
God's marionettes, so when I said,
"What's the difference?, the latter
has us by the long hairs, the former
by the short, the best thing
about Commedia dell'Arte is
improvisation," they said, "There
are only two sides to a question: to
propose a third is treason if true.
Traitors we snatch bald, we
cut off their balls, we set them out
naked on the road to nowheres
as two-bit Abélards, two-bit whores,
and go on arguing as before."

The animals, hanging around in forms,
are each resigned to be what each one is,
imprisoned twice, in flesh first, then in irons.
The Bactrian camel is adjusted or is not
as, with his humps collapsed for lack of need
for water and with useless tufts of hair
like hummocks on the great plains of his flanks,
he stands around in shape and chews
a curd of solace, whether bitter, bland, or sweet,
who knows? Such is his formal pride,
his gargoyle's face remains a stone
assertion as he pisses in between his splayed,
seemingly rachitic legs and stays
that way, in place, for want of something else
to do, caught in his double prison all the time.
Whatever he is, he goes on being what he is,
although ridiculous in forced review,
perseverant in not doing what he need not do.

THE LIFE AND DEATH
OF THE CANTATA SYSTEM

When the Lord was a man of war and sailed out
through the sky at night with all the stars
of all the constellations as his riding lights,
those beneath his oceanic, personal ascendancy
ascended in fated systems. The massed shouts
of the chorus sailed a regular sea of violins
as Galleons of the Line!, with hulls of bassos,
decks of baritones and altos, ornate in poop
and prow in rigging up the masts of soloists
which bore aloft, in turn, soprano mainsails,
topgallants of the children's chorus, and
pennants of castrati streaming on the heights!
The Great Armada sang "Invincible!" to the deep,
but when the time came for a change in craft
the Lord's storms wrecked the vessels of the Lord
and the voices poured out on the air still singing.
The Empirical English conquered in the shallows. He
withdrew his stars to favor those made by machines.

Who knows whether the sea heals or corrodes?
The wading, wintered pack-beasts of the feet
slough off, in spring, the dead rind of the shoes'
leather detention, the big toe's yellow horn
shines with a natural polish, and the whole
person seems to profit. The opposite appears
when dead sharks wash up along the beach
for no known reason. What is more built
for winning than the swept-back teeth,
water-finished fins, and pure bad eyes
these old, efficient forms of appetite
are dressed in? Yet it looks as if the sea
digested what is wished of them with viral ease
and threw up what was left to stink and dry.
If this shows how the sea approaches life
in its propensity to feed as animal entire,
then sharks are comforts, feet are terrified,
but they vacation in the mystery and why not?
Who knows whether the sea heals or corrodes?:
what the sun burns up of it, the moon puts back.

Matter is palsy: the land heaving, water
breaking against it, the planet whirling
days in night. Even at the still point
of night I hear the jockeying for place
of each thing wrestling with itself
to be a wrestler. Is the stress that holds
them, whirling in themselves, an ache?
If so strained to shape and aching for release,
explode to peace! But I am here poised
within this eddy, sentenced to a shape,
and have to wrestle through a gust of violence
before I sleep; so may I make or augment
all these lights at night, so as to give out
all the temporary ornaments I can to peace.

ON FINDING THE
MEANING OF "RADIANCE"

The dreamed Grail found as if in dreams
was not as had been dreamed when found.
The blasted pot, so early in the earth
that it was nearly dirt in dirt, was fired
either in a kiln or a volcano: who can tell
a thumb or tool mark from an earthquake's
pressure in time, and what's the difference?
It is all part of the same process. In
the crater of the natural or potter's pot
there still is some of the first fluid.
It is, and why not say it, Perceval?,
pisslike, with a float of shit on top,
body and blood having changed in time
to what the beasts give back to the ground
with their personalities. Once drained,
the treasure is there in the lees, changed.
The gold filigree, once dreamed to be
a fine vein in the ore with the ore removed,
has run back into its rock, and the gems,
chipped facet by facet from their shells,
are back fast in their stones again, asleep;
but the gold lightning and jewels of fire
are freed in the finding of them, freed
by the nauseous draught: the fire balled
in the skull, the lightning veining the veins.
So I am freed to say, as a piece of dirt
to the body of earth: "Here is where love is,"
and, "This is the meaning of 'Radiance.'"

A GIFT'S ACCOMPANIMENT

The central stone is small, small,
refractive, faceted, and red,
but small because of costs;
oh I can give no larger. Be
distracted from the jewel
which is so small by all
the craft of filigree around it:
it has been worked: it holds
a one night's curiosity
of intertwining stems and leaves,
radiant in ivy from the stone
which is so small. Look at
its corolla: the silvered multiple
details, man-houred craftily
around that stone, are by
love's labors a disguise
of poverty's small heart,
in hopes the saying is a lie
that says: "Small hearts evoke
small fates and no delights."
See how the spider-legged clasp
is soldered practically in back
so you (if you accept it though
the stone, expense, and heart
are small because of costs)
could wear it on the dress
you wear around the chest
you wear around your heart.
Please be the setting of
the setting of the setting of
this heart which is so small
though I can give no larger.

The cut rhododendron branches
flowered in our sunless flat.
Don't complain to me, dear,
that I waste your life in poverty:
you and the cuttings prove: Those
that have it in them to be beautiful
flower wherever they are!, although
they are, like everything else, ephemeral.
Freedom is as mortal as tyranny.

IN THE FOREST

it was warm and cold,
cold from the damps because
it all took place in trees.
When it rained it rained
and when the rain stopped
the trees rained in the wind
and when the trees stopped
it rained. So it went.

Once it was huddling, once
it was sitting apart, once
it was bleeding in time.
We ate and we drank
and we slept and we
did something else
we should not talk about.
Was it love? It was all
supposed to be love.

My it was dark
at night. Whoever it was
who planned that place
forgot the lighting
although some claim to see.

117

I.

Inwardly centered like a child
sucking soda through a straw,
they have their noses in the dirt,
greedily absent, blinded, while
their green behinds in the wind
wave back and forth. Oh I can
hit them and they won't hit back.
Oh let them all come down, slow-
ly at the first inclination from
the vertical, then faster, then
crashing in passion! There is
a hallelujah from the dust and birds,
and insects are set free of hell
in devilish shapes to shrivel in
the solid glare of the day, fools
to the contrary, who maintain
that Christ is down from the heights
by this, to the mother earth again.

2.

It is even, the way the trees,
in coming up from the ground,
from nothing, from a nut,
take liberties in spreading out
like animals, like us. But, brutes
of a chosen ground, they stand

around in suction, dark, grouped
like witnesses afraid to act
beside the accidents of roads
and more afraid to cross except
packed in a squirrel's cheek,
in nuts, or in a fairy's flight
of seed. Their undersides are dark
in contrast to the strong, blond,
human inner arm; even the ground
beneath them is a hairy damp,
dirty as groins. Oh we will cut
them down to boards, pulp, dust,
and size: fury the ax, fury the saw
will cure their spreading stands;
courage will make the world plain.

WHAT THE HELL, RAGE,
GIVE IN TO NATURAL GRACES

She walks. This never has
been done before. She knows
how it is done: her forearms
raised, waving her hands
on the natural rachets of her wrists,
she takes steps! She balances
on black spike heels so sharp
that they would pierce your heart
if she could walk on you,
and smiles to show it off:
this is a giddy new art
she owns squealing because
she steps on certain things—
spittle and cigarette butts
littered from some past—
and comes back from the store
with the first ice-cream cone
in the whole world to date,
her walking being as light
as my irony is heavy.
She blinks rapidly when
she tells me all this because
wild insects of perception get
into her eyes and bite them.
Thinking of history, oh I
must speak of What's-her-name,
sweet sixteen and never been
and never will be, just is;
but speak of love and she's
a sweet one to the senses,

palpably adequate, e-
motionally to be husbanded
because the world is weird
because it's here while she
is. Yesterday would surprise
her if she heard of it,
as will tomorrow when she does,
or else not. As of now,
things are for the first
and last time timeless like
the Classic Comic strips
and known to her agreeably
except for stepped-on things
littered from some past,
so what the hell, rage,
give in to native graces:
her brains are in her tits!,
as she knows bouncingly,
and there for all to love,
since the world fights its war
in her womb and so far wins.

Secular Metamorphosis of Joyce Kilmer's "Trees"

Don't talk to me about trees having branches and roots:
they are all root, except for the trunk, and the high root,
waving its colors in the air, is no less snarled in its food
than is the low root snarled in its specialty: nourishment
in dirt. What with the reciprocal fair trade of the trunk
holding the two roots together and apart in equipoise,
the whole tree stands in solid connection to its whole self
except for the expendable beauty of its seasonal ends,
and is so snarled at either end in its contrary goods
that it studs the dirt to the air with its living wood.
This anagogic significance grows with its growth for years,
twigging in all directions as an evidence of entirety,
although it waves back and forth in the wind and is a host
to fungi, insects, men, birds, and the law of entropy.

POEM

What was once an island with birds,
palms, snakes, and goats in flowers
is now a sand-bar bearing sea clams.
A storm at sea washed over it and it
drowned. There is no food but what
the surf throws up to it and no sweet
water but what the sky throws down.
You are cast away one storm too late
to know the previous ecology,
so may you leave it soon, or fertilize
the sand-bar for another kind of life:
you can do nothing except your part
unless you want a short survival badly.
So what if you act like a storm against
sweet water, other castaways, and clams?
They will give out!, as you will, soon:
no more interrelational elegance
will burgeon on this desert in the sea,
and no prayers make it bear analogies.

MONOLOGUE OF A
COMMERCIAL FISHERMAN

"If you work a body of water and a body of woman
you can take fish out of one and children out of the other
for the two kinds of survival. The fishing is good,
both kinds are adequate in pleasures and yield,
but the hard work and the miseries are killing;
it is a good life if life is good. If not, not.
You are out in the world and in in the world,
having it both ways: it is sportive and prevenient living
combined, although you have to think about the weathers
and the hard work and the miseries are what I said.
It runs on like water, quickly, under the boat,
then slowly like the sand dunes under the house.
You survive by yourself by the one fish for a while
and then by the other afterward when you run out.
You run out a hooky life baited with good times,
and whether the catch is caught or not is a question
for those who go fishing for men or among them for things."

VARIATION ON A
THEME BY STEVENS

In fall and whiskey weather when
the eye clears with the air and blood
comes up to surface one last time
before the winter and its sleeps,
the weeds go down to straws,
the north wind strips most birds
out of the atmosphere and they
go southward with the sunlight,
the retired people, and rich airs.
All appetites revive and love
is possible again in clarity
without the sweats of heat: it makes
warmth. The walleyed arctic birds
arrive to summer in the fall,
warmed by these chills; geese
practice their noisy Vs,
half a horizon wide, and white owls
hide from their crows in the pines.
Therefore it is not tragic to stay
and not tragic or comic to go,
but it is absolutely typical to say
goodbye while saying hello.

FROM ROME. FOR MORE PUBLIC FOUNTAINS IN NEW YORK CITY

Oh effervescent palisades of ferns in drippage,
the air sounds green by civic watered bronze
fountains in New York City. Hierarchs of spray
go up and down in office: they scour the noons
when hot air stinks to itself from Jersey's smoke
and the city makes itself a desert of cement.
Moses! Command the sun to august temperance!
When water rises freely over force and poises,
cleaning itself in the dirty air, it falls back
on the dolphins, Poseidon, and moss-headed nymphs,
clean with the dirt of air left cleansed by its
clear falling, and runs down coolly with the heat
to its commune, pooling. What public utility!
The city that has working fountains, that lights
them up at night electrically, that does not say
to thirsters at its fountains: DO NOT DRINK!—
that city is well ordered in its waters and drains
and dresses its corruption up in rainbows, false
to the eye but how expressive of a cool truth being.
The unitary water separates, novel on its heights,
and falls back to its unity, discoursing. So let
New York City fountains be the archives of ascent
that teach the low high styles in the open air
and frondage of event! Then all our subway selves
could learn to fall with grace, after sparkling,
and the city's life acknowledge the water of life.

ACCOMMODATION TO DETROIT

"When good people die they become worms in Detroit," they say.
"When bad people die they go to Hamtramck just as they are."
It is all right to mock it, but some are exalted: they
have escape to the cities from the badlands to the south
and see them as their Edens found, with Eves and the fruits
and shelter under iron trees. They have had a hard life
as draught animals, and are here to try out human life,
temptations first. They are walled away from their wilderness
by absence in stone and iron, the way Hamtramck is walled
by Detroit, city in city, cement in cement, and seed in shell.
Greater Detroit is what has grown around the ones who have
Hamtramck or nothing as a preview of a concrete flower to come.

TO PARIS: FEAR OF THE
HEIGHTS REACHED

Oh I came up from anywhere
from underground, brushing the dirt
from my hair and knees, and climbed
the long stalk of the road until
it flowered in confusing petals. I
thought I was lost in its light
shadows, in confusion of ways
and absence of felt pattern. I hoped
to find a way back out again
but was so lost I found
the heart, place, square, monoliths, and fountains
bleeding with honey out of which the city grew,
bowing away in plan, petal on petal,
as a chrysanthemum of sunlight.
Oh I felt out its day's commitment
to the sun, and how it shone itself
throughout one night. There was
the sky above it, high although
the flower of the city was up high.
Oh I stayed out the cycle of its day,
drunk on its juices, sneezing its dust,
and shaken by the order and complexity.
I was convinced that it was beautiful
but left it: it was not for me,
so I came off it and am back
down where I came from on the ground.

STABILITY BEFORE DEPARTURE

I have begun my freedom and it hurts.
Time opens out, so I can see its end
as the black rock of Mecca up ahead.
I have cut loose from my bases of support
and my beasts and burdens are ready, but
I pace back and forth across my right
of way, shouting, "Take off! Move out
in force!", but nothing moves. I wait
for a following storm to blast me out of here
because to go there freely is suicide!
Let the wind bear my responsibility.

Outside it is cold. Inside,
although the fire has gone out
and all the furniture is burnt,
it is much warmer. Oh let
the white refrigerator car
of day go by in glacial thunder:
when it gets dark, and when
the branches of the tree outside
look wet because it is so dark,
oh we will burn the house itself
for warmth, the wet tree too,
you will burn me, I will burn you,
and when the last brick of the fireplace
has been cracked for its nut of warmth
and the last bone cracked for its coal
and the andirons themselves sucked cold,
we will move on!, remembering
the burning house, the burning tree,
the burning you, the burning me,
the ashes, the brick-dust, the bitter iron,
and the time when we were warm,
and say, "Those were the good old days."

POEMS 3

I fell away toward death
for lack of company and goods:
no business but to flinch.
A woman caught me with the hook
her smile wore at its edge
and wound me up with a winch.
Love's bucket, I was refilled!
So I came back and kissed
and cursed her. She fixed lunch.
She gave me solid grounds,
the company of laughter,
and the water works. Oh I
recant! I should invest
in fly-by-night concerns
while I have flesh to risk
and currency to burn,
so I will hang around
her wellhead and decant
death's water to my drawer.

You	Where I came from is torn down,
say,	where I'm at is condemned,
"You	and where I'm going to
can't	is not built up yet. My Grand
be	Father steamed away from yours
any	for eats! regards! and joys.
good	Better to be Dugan the Cop
because	and never talk about a shitty past
you	than to be classed out
aren't	of the potatoes in the old
some	sod. He dreamed America up, and I
one	played Indian against
from	his cowboy lies because:
some	tradition is for the rich
place."	to love, the clerks
Ha!	to ape, the poor
	to suffer, so I wander
	to take the air, regards, and joys.
	Where are they? You
	will tell me. Anyone
	free of your slavery
	is better off in his own,
	so Up the five-hour day!
	Up art! Up the I.R.A.!

AGAINST A SICKNESS: TO THE
FEMALE DOUBLE PRINCIPLE GOD

She said: "I'm god and all
of this and that world and love
garbage and slaughter all the time
and spring once a year. Once a year
I like to love. You can adjust
to the discipline or not,
and your sacrificial act
called 'Fruitfulness in Decay'
would be pleasing to me
as long as you did it with joy.
Otherwise, the prayer 'Decay,
Ripe in the Fruitfulness'
will do if you have to despair."

Prayer

You know that girl of yours
I liked? The one with strong legs,
grey eyes, weak in the chest
but always bouncing around?
The one they call "The Laugh,"
"The Walk," "That Cunt," "The Brain,"
"Talker, Talker, Talker," and
"The Iron Woman"? Well,
she's gone, gone gone, gone
gone gone to someone else,
and now they say that she,
"My Good," "My True," "My Beautiful,"

is sick to her god-damned
stomach and rejects all
medication. What do you do
to your physical praisers that
they fall apart so fast
or leave me? She needs help now,
yours or that prick's,
I don't know which.

    "I have worked out
    my best in belief
    of the rule, 'The best
    for the best results
    in love of the best,'
    or, 'To hell with it:
    I am just god:
    it's not my problem.' "

I will sit out this passion
unreconciled, thanks: there are
too many voices. My visions
are not causal but final:
there's no place to go to
but on. I'll dance at the ends
of the white strings of nerves
and love for a while, your slave.
Oh stupid condition, I drink
to your Presences in hope of sleep
asleep, and continuity awake.

What do you do if you meet a witch?
Move! from the scenery of belief in her
by air, by car, by foot, by back-
roads if you must, but move! Leave!
And if you can't or think you can't,
Oh build a fort of reason in her country,
and walk the battlements of stone,
of brick, of mud, of sticks, of thorn-
bush if you lack, and say the charm:
"2 plus 2 is four," a truth so true
it laughs: "Tautology! Tautology!" before
the numbers change in speech and come
in screams, in shouts, in lalling, or
in curses if you hurt. 2 plus 2
is Noah's Ark, with every couple in it
coupled into one and crying differently
to make a third, a fourth, a fifth, a litter.
Dove, find us a land of peace and ease.
Come back with a bomb or burning bough
proof in your claws that love or death,
in giving us the business, gives us all.

A man applying gold leaf
to the window's word backwards
combed his hair to charge
his gilder's tip with static,
so he charged his hair with gold.
He was electrically the gold-
haired father of the gold word
GOODS! and god of the store's
attractions. When he waved his maul-
stick I went in to buy
the body of his mystery.

NOT TO CHOOSE

I should be someplace else!,
but pace around in the sweats
of inhumane endeavor and its trash:
goods, deeds, credits, debts.
Have it your own way, life:
I'm just here to die, but I
would rather live it out as a fool
and have a short life in contempt
and idle graces, but, instead,
the office telephone goes off
and voices out of its dark night
command me, "Choose, Choose,"
while women's angel voices call
the cities and their numbers. Then,
when I do choose: "I run away!"
the shop door opens and a cop
or statue stands there in the way.
What does he want? Blood. Oh
let me tumble in the wards, bolts,
and chambers of a police lock locked
so I can get to sleep again,
warm in the guaranteed steel!
Instead, I have to fake him off
with promises to pay. Cash!
How cold action is. I should
do spiritual exercises toward
the body of this world
and get in shape for choices,

choices, No! Instead, I leave
the dirty business by the back
window, climb down the fire escape,
and sneak off out of town alive
with petty cash and bad nerves in
an old Ford with a broken muffler!
So here I am again, July,
vacationing in your country broke,
in debt, not bankrupt yet!
and free to get your message!
What is it?
To begin again in another state!

Ah to be alone and uninhibited!
To make mistakes in private, then
to show a good thing! But that's
not possible: it's in the Close of life
that towering Virtù happens. Why
be absent from the wheeling world?
It is an education! Act by act,
Futures materialize! So, go deal,
old bones, enjoy it while you may!:
eat, drink, think, and love; oh even work!,
as if all horrors are mistakes,
and make the social product: new
invisible skies arriving! full
of life, death, insanity, and grace!

The red curtain moving in the still room
is frightening in portent to me housed.
The heart, in its choice cage of ribs, pounds
as if the air, which was a hurricane
all up the dangerous Atlantic coast
with gross waves and accumulative clouds,
has petered out into an indoor draught
telling the officed brain, high up inside
the dead air of its hairy capitol dome
but sensitive as a bat to every draught,
that revolutionary storms are happening down there!
to move the red curtain in the still room.

The old road followed
the lay of the land
to fords. It went
commercially to towns
around it, curving
in respect to rocks
and skirting pastures,
but the Imperial Road
denied the map relief
and spanned its rapids.
It crossed and climbed,
regardless of contour,
straight as a weapon
should be. Now,
with both disused,
and armed pilgrims
walking cross-country
to avoid the air's
condors and fliers, who
can say which road
travelled the better
to what end, or how
the travelling was
that got us nowhere,
under hell's angels.

There is smoke over the river at the end of the street.
Something is happening, because the air is full of news.
An arriver or departer is arriving or departing and
displaces tons of water up against the rotten piers.
The gutters run with it. I hope that she or it
will bring or take a cargo of the manifest goods
and not that plague that goes from there to here
or here to there in rats' nests in the bilge beneath
the blue and white flag of the Scandinavian sky.

Hide in cesspools, sleep well
on broken glass, and eat
shit. Kiss the whips,
hold the wife for rape,
and have good luck:
stumble behind a lamb
before the bomb bursts
and crawl out of the wreck
to be the epitaph:
"The good ones die first,
but I am not so bad:
Americans are worse."

What do a few crimes
matter in a good life?
Adultery is not so bad.
You think yourself too old
for loving, gone in the guts
and charms, but a woman says,
"I love you," a drunken lie,
and down you go on the grass
outside the party. You rejoin
the wife, delighted and renewed!
She's grateful but goes out
with a bruiser. Blood
passions arise and die
in lawyers' smiles, a few
children suffer for life,
and that's all. But: One
memo from that McNamara and his band
can kill a city of lives
and the life of cities, too,
while L.B. "Killer" Johnson And His Napalm Boys
sit singing by their fire:
The Goldberg Variations.
So, what do a few crimes
matter in a neutral life?
They pray the insignificance
of most private behavior.

The man who first saw nothing
drew a line around it
shaped like a kiss or gasp
or any of the lips' expressions during shock,
and what had been interior
welled from its human source
and pooled, a mirror perilous.
That was the mouth of the horn of agony,
the womb all matter tumbled out of in the first
meaningless avalanche of the concrete,
and I'm afraid that it will be
the sewer of all water and the grave of space
so as to be complete.

When his head, dead tired of its theory,
dropped to the mark it made,
his forehead drank the kiss of nothing.
That was not sleep!
His students dove through it
down oceans of absence and
are not remembered, but
beautiful wet women ran out of the surf, subtly changed
and laughing over something secret they had learned.
Their navigating sons
sailed past horizons of the sensed
and founded wonderlands!
deep in the deserts of flesh away
from heaven's waters. They have not returned either.

I am not interested in mathematics
as a way of knowing, but
once I was the bravest acrobat
ever to leap through burning hoops!
Now I balk when I run at
my burning mirror, mouth, and twin,
afraid that I will not break out again
the other side of death,
applauded, unscorched, and agrin.
Oh I refuse that lovers' leap
through spit and image
down the throat of shock
and into the opposite day.
I am afraid that parity is lost
and nothing wins.

Once I calmed
myself before that chaos caught
so weakly in the charms of will
and called it cornucopia, cloaca, or else: nought;
but now the charmed
circle seems no longer to be charmed;
its wizards must have lost
the mumbo-jumbo that could call up
useful salamanders, fiends, and witches from the pit
and hold them helpless in the will
and tractable to Liberal errands.

Now when the fouls appear
howling and snorting fire,
who is to ride them out
fairly and full of honor like the knights
and to what businesses?
Whole governments of them
induce it at the world's heart,
all their citizens are food,
and it can drink the oceans,
eat the mountains, roots to peaks,
and bubble to the outer edge of air
to be a nova. "Istimirant Stella!"
strangers might say, and make their own
unearthly, efficient prophecies.

After sleepers first touch zero at the maw
they wake up in a permanently different light.
They wear its caste-mark as another eye
incapable of sleep or hurt, and burrowing inside.
They're fed to it; it
widens unastonished and they drown: internally.
If only I knew a woman's charm I cannot learn
in whose clear form and lines
the trouble of the problem slept, solved,
oh they would have a lid against its light,
rest in the mystery, and a chance
blindly to venture on in time,

but no such Cyclops
crazed by the price of size
would search the bellies of his sheep
to thank his blinders and their flame-sharp stick;
his eye is the condition of his flock
and his flock is his food and fleece;
so: sack the world's
unfinished business in your balls,
Ulysses, and escape
to soaking Venus or the red plains
of Mars: Nothing might be here.

POEM

What's the balm
for a dying life,
dope, drink, or Christ,
is there one?

I puke and choke
with it and find
no peace of mind
in flesh, and no hope.

It flows away
in mucous juice.
Nothing I can do
can make it stay,

so I give out
and water the garden: it
is all shit
for the flowers anyhow.

"Courage!" I say. Thus exhorting myself,
I say encouraging words the way the lame
Tyrtaeus was supposed to have been paid
to say them, making marching songs to make
whole Spartans march away in whole faith:

> "Now hear this, you sons
> of Hercules: God is on
> our side, so make believe
> black death is white as day.
> Dress up your hair for war
> as if for girls or boys
> and throw your bodies away:
> Love and your death are equal joys."

But in his own crippled song to himself,
"On Marching Lamely," he paid himself to say:

> "Go it alone, kid.
> Run your own races.
> But when they say, 'Shit!'
> squat and make faces."

All these men later died. His and their fame
goes on in all military routines,
while the counter-song I make him say
of army verse I've said and heard
goes on in enlisted men's latrines.

LET HEROES ACCOUNT TO LOVE

Statement   *Accounting*

I too was born out of a lion's mouth
and have the twenty-one longitudinal marks
of passage through the teeth to prove it:
Oh I am split up the middle half way,   1 slice
and once up either side, further up.   2 slices
These four strips got split up into fives each   8 slices
at their tips, since once the head was out   for the fingers
and chewed to features, then the teeth   8 slices
began to close, firmly: they clenched   for the toes
around the fingers and the toes. I pulled out!
But where the main cut of the center teeth
began, oh it is ragged and still hurts   2 slices
or wants or hopes, I don't know which,   for the penis
and strives to grow together in a whole.   (the
It's stiff in tantrum with this wish   balls
from time to time, since I was what was all   fell
there was inside the lionskin when I shucked it,   dual
and would come to you, love, past divides.   in
So when you see some hero's face   desire
framed in a lion's jaws and teeth,   later
do not be so impressed by valor's clothing.   on.)
Beast's puke, let him endure the tortures of undress. —
Vomit your essence, Hercules. Be me: 21

TWO HATREDS OF ACTION

1. Hero

If I were in the belly of the whale
I'd praise the peristalsis of my death
and play the bleeding cilia, I felt,
like clappers of my hopes' carillon! But
once I have been downed I find
the swimming hard in acid, hard among
the downed ferocities of sharks,
my swallowed brothers, so I war
with the living dead. Terror of peace
swallows the praise, because my parts
will go to feed the beast. Sharks and I,
once we have chewed identity to shreds,
will be Leviathan, the that which eats
the carnivores in combat through its bowels.
Sleep in its body and blood! That's all
the stomach joy there is among toothed souls.

2. Coward

I won a precious I
from selfless sleep. The bells,
whistles, and alarms of dawn
awoke me. Oh I was scared
and hung around in hell:
an Idyll. Then the flags
and brass band of the day
began to fly. The opted I
was drafted and fell in

behind the chest-boom of the drum
or public heart. I drummed within
and marched away, while my true love,
who gave the word to start,
ran weeping by my side.
Fifes drilled through my ears
and found my trouble: brains
coiled in the greys of self,
and reamed them with the shrieks
of civic cadence. Forward! I
was forced to march,
up to the point of fire! Halt!:
Did I win out of sleep
just to be worked and slain?
No! Oh I would rather sleep
well out of uniform,
be slapped and shouted at
by officers of the day,
and win my death at ease,
not in the army game!
but I say what the drum says:
boom. The fifes squeal WE.
My brains are drummed out
of the corpse and wheedled away.

Mother!, I am sick
of alcohol and grown up
foods. That blue milk
diet that I used to suck
is what I need. If you
give up your sour weeds
I will tear out
my permanently biting teeth
so we can be attached
again as sucker-shark
and shark, I mouthless on
you, and you savagely mouthed.
Oh we will course the Deeps
as pure efficiencies
where life obeys its first
imperative of desire: eat!,
and not the second: screw!
Oh I will close my eyes
so tight they disappear
in trusting sleep: who needs
them? Wills. Lovers. You.

I closed my ears with stinging bugs
and sewed my eyelids shut
but heard a sucking at the dugs
and saw my parents rut.

I locked my jaw with rusty nails
and cured my tongue in lime
but ate and drank in garbage pails
and said these words of crime.

I crushed my scrotum with two stones
and drew my penis in
but felt your wound expect its own
and fell in love with sin.

EXPENSES

I choked my frog on human crumbs.
My mother fainted when she saw
a toadstool growing from my thumb
and would not let me out of doors.
I drowned lead soldiers in the sink.
My parents fought a war downstairs.
My father lost me with a wink,
and grey pushed out his chocolate hair.
I found the toilet much too late
and stole away on roller skates,
hoping to find a cheaper law
behind the penny candy store.
I have the honor, love, to be
your animal, but will not please.

THE BUTCHER!, BORGES, WHAT A SHOCK!

—for Donald Mark Fall

*We have been well
and truly had.—Pascal*

What a jewel the view
is from the furnished room,
flashing with red, green,
and orange traffic lights:
That's dancing!, and it sings
as a general sound. What
a crystal air is,
metrical in structure,
clear in the open-work,
burning at its joints,
and moving in its bodies ordered everywhere
as force's products in pure chance.
What an honor to be in it,
even as a flaw, Oh
fracture of a tree in solid quartz!

Oh I had to look away
and down the open trap-
door in the center of the room,
into the cellar hole
where I have not yet fallen.
The man-faced bat-winged worm
looked up from his work
on my love's corpse falling,
his grin foul with his lights,
and said, "So what?, Faller,
I come in the works
of your love's wounds, foaming.
My sperm are his worms."

Love, I have known
you in your change
from spring to garbage, so
I ask you: Why
is the world so beautiful?

It has to be all sex
to make us want it here
against the worm's brief:
"I am the root and teeth.
What you dream I am.
You are the meat.
Fly if you can."

So: Beget sons against death.
Get real estates against decay,
and praise physical glory!:

The stars above the roof
are there as God's dust
at the center of this sphere
whose edge is nowhere.

—from "Pascal's Sphere"
by Jorge Luis Borges.

POEM

The Pythagorean Silences
opted for the flesh
and came and burned in it.
They thought, felt, and watched,
wanting some ecstasy.
Oh unaccountable spirits,
they take this on as choice,
get fated, and become,
out of their nothingness,
cropping summer of delight.
They like to burn in the sun.
There is, oh nervousness,
no granary at night:
the flying chaff of the stars
should demonstrate this thesis.
They like this life and death
and stare out of the stone
forehead of a horse
as if it were some sport.

ON GAINING A SOUL

As I explained the rules,
quarters, and conveniences,
the bloodless animal
I'll call "my soul"
tongued at my blackest tooth
in absent-minded joy
and asked about the truth
of feeling: it has a short
vacation in the flesh
and everything to do,
so I should take great pains
to satisfy the guest
so that it does not leave
before I make it pay.

ON A SNAKE

The snake on the blue
pool table of the moss
is denser than a stick
of equal girth and heavier,
for all its lightness and
slick ways, because its
muscles organized beneath
the overlapping platelets of
oiled parchment have to be
compact to make that tense
wobble of reaction that
you feel if you should pick
it up. Now that I know
the motto: DON'T TOUCH SNAKES,
and wear the diacritical marks
the two fangs make, I say,
"Man, you are smarter than it,
that muscular intelligence:
snap off its head!" The glass
snake, weighty and complex
in otherness, must think
the whole thought of the cold
when it is cold. He would
not know the drag end
of his tail from twigs
around him in the snow
when you are wiser warm,
dreaming of venom by the fire
where a cautery instrument
turns red, and healing rum
roars when the poker is dipped in.

The color of the sac and stinger of the scorpion
was red, and got its beauty from their poison. Bare
feet ache with the threat, the eyes with praise,
the serum for revulsion. Praise be, then, that
the armored teardrop searching on the tail
could miss feet, sting sight, and reconcile
death's stamping panic with a vision of form,
red at the point where chance and law join.

IDYLL OF ASCENSION

Clicking in rock pasturage,
the deer were delicate except
for grass sounds in their teeth
from nervous grazing.

Rightly addicted to shock,
fangless economies like these
mooing advocates of speed
posit a lion in ambush;

lying down with him
in ravin's daily dream,
they struggle out of flesh
under his padded paw.

"I am undone," sings the lion,
and leaps. His Worship
drinks at the throat's race,
swills in the hollow gut

spilling with sweets, sick
with private desire, and takes
the pasture-price for flesh:
his noble joy in rending.

So it all goes, upward
like the deer's pop eyes;
whoever devours the lion
tastes the deer's flavor.

ON A HYMN, MISPRINTED

Oh they were doing custom
slaughtering down Dead End Road.
Because I am a soldier of the Gross
I went to see
the soldier of the Lamb
get his. Such eyes!
such chops! such skin!
Oh shall I fear to own the cause
or blush to speak its name?
No! It's Murder! Murder!
I sail through bloody seas.

BRUTALIZATION UNDER THE HEART OF PEACE

After the engagement they stacked their arms,
wrapped their hunger in the old stains
of lousy bandages, and fought themselves asleep
beneath a white-flowering tree.
Its bark was black with clear rain.
The red heart of peace, pecked at by a dove,
hung hidden by the flowers on a high branch
the way a ham is hung up from the dogs
to cure. Why hang a heart up
in the white disguises of a black-barked tree?
The birds will get it. Also: flowers fail: once
shaken harmonically by shots or shouts,
they fall together, or they shrivel in the stench
rising from the soldiers' dirty sleep
and fall to bare the red peace of heart.
Irregulars, arisen frightened in white rain,
go jump for it, grinning like dogs
because of want. They shoot it down
as an edible beast, or as a target, or
as something else to shoot. They make
their wounds gape and utter fearful cries.
They make the bird fly off for other forage.

POEM

The tree was wet with the moon's
red water when two souls
came down from flight outside the air.

They cried at the fall to flesh
among the snapping dogs on land
and the crawfish in the water

by the tree. Their cries condensed and held
as one dove on and one heart hung
from two different branches. The white dove sang

its love of hearts; the heart
wept blood at its danger. The night
turned blue to be the moon's lungs,
and the red tree its bronchia.

POEM

Oh that was not a scrap of flying Daily News
falling on the wind
that some kid caught
and held up laughing from a snapping dog:
That was the dove itself come down
to be the pigeon for the day
when captured love grows up
to any life it has in goods and children.

The child signed the steamed pane
with his nose and fingerprints. He drew
a heart's shape, the initials
of a beautiful stranger, and his own,
pierced by an arrow that was clear and cold.
The power of his waiting changed
to light: the lights came on
inside and out, it was so strong,
and then the smell of women, food,
and household pee was changed. Cloth
came in with short whiskers soaked
in beer, tobacco-smoke and air-
smells from the business of outside.
Strength moved through the rooms
laughing too loud and hard
for the long bead curtains of rules
around explosive plates and cracking chairs.
First as a marsupial of pockets, then
as a freehold bird swung in the air,
his knowledge of the world of god
expanded in a space too small for joy.

ON ALEXANDER AND ARISTOTLE, ON A
BLACK-ON-RED GREEK PLATE

The linear, encircled youth
acclaimed his limits running
in the bottom of a plate
with "he's a handsome lad"
scratched anyhow around
him as a joke or hint
of love. A northern prince,
finishing his cereal beneath
a Grecian tutor's smile,
would see the one clear line
appear, become a youth,
and run off on the way
from breakfast to the city
through an alphabet
circumferenced by art.
This is doubt's breakfast
in a school of Gordian knots:
in ending at the genitals,
where it began, the line
is doubled on itself and tied
unclearly in a bow knot
with dangles. The lewd
scratches mar design well.
Which way can princes turn
with The Philosopher behind
them and the Greeks in front?

If cooks can shatter art
then love is menial, and boys
can use it to be gods
in thirty-some-odd years.
That was doubt's breakfast
in the school of Gordian tricks:
"To have good government
thinkers should form the king,"
so when he took his way
he took Real armies with him:
Athens crumbled in the Seen
of Alexander's sober frown
and tricked his looking to go on
to Porus and the elephants
and drunkenness in Babylon.

NIGHT SONG FOR A BOY

Lock up the church,
I feel as unasleep
as a dead cat: regards
are what I want,
regards, regards, regards.
A priest after boy's ass
feels better than I
do: When I walk around
ladies on the stoops
think I am death: If I
had steel plates on my heels
Oh they would know it.
I should rape a saint
and she could save me
from the dangers of life.

FOR LISA

May flowers of dirt and
flowers of rocketry both
be in your bunch, love,
when you get married out
beyond my death to you
and the world's wars.
Agreed! Oh she agrees
to anything for laughs,
love, and being danced
to records playing dances.

ADVERTISING IN PARIS

On the old bridge, the bridge
they call "New Bridge,"
a model wearing the brassiere
named "Triumph!" posed
on the archaic stone.
Novelty and persistence meet
in formal beauty
and what wins? The river.

The smell in the diamond morning was
of a restaurant cleaning up. Two men
carried a container full of slops
to a commercial garbage truck
and drove the night-time tares away
once appetite had made the day.

Portage of day from night to night,
I had hoped to sit in the staring sun
at bitter ease, cool in the tares
of will, and also wonder how to be
not part of it, the cartage, slops,
and increments of day. Who is to eat

with such an attitude?, wooing the world
with claims. Porters and their freights
form in the aches, so I must carry three
pieces of paper and a ball-point pen
from one desk to another for profit
while there is profit under the sun.

POEM

Always prudent but unprepared
for spontaneity in weather,
the office workers got their pressed
survival jackets soaked
while running in new rain
from work to travel home.
Some of the typists laughed
to feel real water not
from taps: they are the ones
with joys to dream of, once
the day is typed away. Once
I'd hoped to dream in the rain
for life, unbothered by
the economics of appearance,
and I did, for years, and knew
its soaking intimacy. Now
I'm pressed in the synthetics too,
and have no place to go
to in the weather, except home,
but it is not so bad,
pacing an empty office after 5
in the trash of squalid crises.
I hit the key of "I"
on a girl's machine, and see
that it is red, nail polish red,
with her device of getting on
beautifully for survival:
that is not just vanity!
I get rebellious for the truth
of outside weather often, but
my check is here each Friday.

The day is full of people, Sun,
walking around the staring noon
of paid endeavor: it is a shock
to someone who has slept apart
all morning in a shaded room
to come out into traffic. I
am hopelessly in arrears. I try
to catch up on the action, eat
a lunch for breakfast and pretend:
What have I missed except life?

POEM

A man with a box walked up to a woman with a boy, gave the box
to the boy, said, "Don't drop it for a change," and kissed
the woman, sucking up her rosebud from her mud-color. It bloomed.
He said, "Let's go." They went, with technicolor haloes of the usual
around them. Why? Because: They come from a star, live by its light,
and burn with it here in the dark outside of the department store.

I came out on the wrong
side of time and saw
the rescue party leave.
"How long must we wait?"
I said. "Forever. You
are too far gone to save,
too dangerous to carry off
the precipice, and frozen stiff
besides. So long. You
can have our brandy. That's life."

ON RAPE UNATTEMPTED

"Be alive," they say, when I
am so alive I ache with it
so much I do not look alive
but chase that cock-teaser till
my balls so ache with her
that I fall groaning into speech
and write the one word RAPE
on subway lavatory walls
while she, receptive but to me,
dances and sings around me:
"Yes and no and maybe so
and everywhere all over." Oh
my nonsense: she's the truth;
I cry the sentence of the Fool:
"I don't know what to do!"
Her left eye winks Yes,
her right eye stares No,
and her smile smiles smiles
while I write copy for
her disappearance on the air!
as "Miss Unknowable, 1964."

If I were out of love
and sequence I would turn
the end of love—its death—
knifelike against myself
to cut off my distinction and
rejoin the Commons, maimed.
But love is here!, so by
that contact with the one
oh may I contact all
self-alienated aliens
in Atom City and apply
to join the one big union.
Workers of this world, unite!

Once, when I liked a German girl,
hating the Krauts but loving the tongue
in a loving mouth, I'd make her say
"Apple!" that crucial word, and feel
like Tenzing and Hillary on Everest,
   breathless and drinking hot lemonade
     to a victory dried out of nationalism,
      class, and caste, and drunken back
        to the Garden's original purity on the heights!
Later I lapsed into hate and lost
the taste of her mouth in division.

on horseback, and
the saber's drawn,
lunar acuity
cut out a slice
of sunlight in mid-air.
He whirled it once
around his head, a halo, and
discharged it at a foe.
Charge forever, hero! Rear,
horse! The saber points
toward death, by means
of which he changed
into a statue in the square.
To you the glory, brother,
and to us the girls.

NARCISSUS II

I used to beg for roses in the garden of love
and got them. The couples laughed and paid.
Not any more. Now the ladies do not smile.
Their gentlemen draw swords and order me away.
I went to look in Narcissus' public pool,
weeping and asking why. I had a beard! I saw,
and heard the answer: "Figure it out for yourself:
you must have grown up blind to be a fool.
Isn't there something you should want to do
or die?" "Oh remarkable absence of joy, what is it?"
A sword broke surface toward me, point first.
Then her hand around the hilt appeared,
and then herself, smiling. "Here it is," she said,
"from point to hilt and hand: take it either way."

POEM

It is no wonder that new lovers run
rice gantlets to Niagara Falls
or to some other elephant wonder:
once weightless love finds bodying
in the archaic landscapes of the flesh
it needs proportion in its flow
and goes to public waters. There
it falls asleep unoverwhelmed
while fall sounds shake the panes
of Sweetheart Cottages & Darling Hotel,
and wakes up ordinarily disposed to say:
"I gained ten pounds!", "We never got
to see the Falls!", or, "All is well."

Oh put the elephant in chains.
His must is dangerous.
Three tons of love in pain
run trumpeting over us.

POEM

Flowering balls!,
roses are coming on
in solar systems oh
galactic rose bush. By
tomorrow, given rain,
roses will be out for bees.
It's yours and mine, wild
rose, to open to for love,
its stingers and its rain,
but it is Its always.

The birth of Seventh Avenue
from Varick Street at night
is out of surf, all moonshine
as it breaks along the curb,
coming, flooding, and falling away.
In it, matter's savagery
extrudes a civic fault, a man
wading in moonlight blocks
away, hunchbacked in the shape
of things before my birth,
beyond my death, and now,
panicked by night alive.
I fear the animal embrace
of Venus' negative half-
creature of the universe,
whose wildness, let in out of love,
must be the genius of this place.

SAILING TO JERUSALEM

On coming up on deck Palm Sunday morning, oh
we saw the seas the dancy little tourist ship
climbed up and down all night in cabin dreams.
They came along in ridges an horizon wide!
and ran away astern to the Americas we left,
to break on headlands and be called "the surf."
After services below, the pilgrims to the east
carried their processed palm fronds up on deck
and some of them went overboard from children's hands.
So, Christ: there were the palm leaves on the water
as the first fruits of the ocean's promised land.
They promise pilgrims resurrection out at sea,
though sea-sick fasters in their bunks below
cry out for harbor, order, and stability.
This is the place for it! The sky is high
with it, the water deep, the air its union: spray!
We all walk the water just below the decks
too, helplessly dancing to the world's variety
like your Jerusalem, Byzantium, and Rome.

Now that autumn is over and all
that increase has been reaped or wasted,
a dead tree and the dead vines on it
scrape together in the wind as strings and bows.
This is so it can be said of listeners:
"They heard playing," before the snow
falls thicker and thicker until the air
is all snow. Then, when we dig out
of it into the upper air, those sounds
will have been buried from the air
and we will hear the silence above the tree.
This is so it can be said of listeners:
"They heard silence," not: "They never heard
a thing about the music underneath them."

Two main diseases, con-
sciousness and dreams, demand
it, a division of the whole.
Then   Then
the   around   the
flesh   the   mind
weeps   speech-   weeps
to   less   to
itself   center: itself
alone   alone
That by this simple split
the subtler be rejoined: then
flesh sings in its throat,
the speechless center spreads
its wings, and Nothing says
an eagle! taking sustenance
from animals of the ground.

The broken glass on the stairs
shines in the electric light.
Whoever dropped the beer
was anti-social or too drunk
to sweep it up himself.
So the beauty goes, ground
under heel but shining, it
and the deposit lost. But
by the janitor's broom
it is still sharp enough
for dogs' feet, babies' hands,
and eyes pierced by its lights,
that he should curse the fool
and I should try to praise
the pieces of harmony.

I have found my figures,
love, and I am theirs
to do with as we will.
Oh they got sucked into the void
spaces of an infant skull
because a storm blew up in there
around a cataclysm: birth.
They fought as winged lions
until they fouled the waste
with carrion and living jaws
and almost died: their ghosts
still roar around on the air
above the desert floor
but leave objective room,
lamb, for your material:
love. Oh it is here
that I propose to build
it, the cathedral "Abattoir":
it is a concrete fold, in plan,
with columned lions to mark
it, set in a desert storm.
Please be its visitor.